A PROVEN SYSTEM TO GET MORE CLIENTS, WIN MORE BUSINESS, AND GROW YOUR CONSULTING FIRM

NEVER CHASE CLIENTS AGAIN

MICHAEL MOSHIRI

FORMER DELOITTE, EY, AND PWC EXECUTIVE REVEALS THE BUSINESS DEVELOPMENT STRATEGIES OF THE WORLD'S BIGGEST CONSULTING FIRMS

Copyright © 2015 by Michael Moshiri. All rights reserved. Except as permitted under the United States Copyright Act of 1976, no part of this publication may be reproduced, transmitted, downloaded, decompiled, reverse engineered, or stored in or introduced into any information storage and retrieval system, in any form or by any means, whether electronic or mechanical, now known or hereinafter invented, without the express written permission of the Publisher.

Published by Pivora, Inc. in the United States. Requests to the Publisher should be addressed to the Permissions Department, Pivora, Inc., 3317 E Bell Road, Suite 101-200, Phoenix, AZ 85032, or via electronic mail at support@pivora.com.

This publication is designed to provide accurate and authoritative information in regard to the subject matter it covers. It is sold with the understanding that the Publisher and Author are not engaged in rendering professional services. If professional advice or other expert assistance is required, the services of a competent professional should be obtained.

ISBN: 978-0-9963944-2-0

10 9 8 7 6 5 4 3 2 1

To my mother and late father
for their never-ending support and love.

To Diana, my wife and soul mate
for always believing in me.

Contents

Acknowledgements	9
Introduction	13
How to Use This Book	17
PART ONE: PREPARE FOR SUCCESS	**21**
Why Many Consultants Fail	23
Three Core Qualifications	35
PART TWO: FIND HIGHLY QUALIFIED CLIENTS	**57**
The Client Catalyst System	59
Step 1. Establish Criteria	65
Step 2. Evaluate Catalysts	79
Step 3. Engage Catalysts	97
Step 4. Elevate Yourself	109
Step 5. Explore Opportunities	125

PART THREE: STAY COMPETITIVE 133

Why Practice Does Not Make Perfect 135
Conclusion 143

Appendix A: Summary of Online Resources 147
Appendix B: The Client Catalyst System Quick Reference 151
Notes 153
Index 155
About the Author 163

Acknowledgements

Although finishing this book has been my obsession from the moment the thought of writing it crossed my mind, it would have never seen the light of day without the help, feedback, and encouragement of an array of amazing people.

Roin Nance

I am eternally grateful to you, my friend and mentor, for teaching me so much about excellence in consulting and about building extraordinary client relationships.

Ken DeJarnette

I am forever thankful to you for guiding and encouraging me to believe in myself and in my ability to build a successful consulting firm. Without your keen advice, I would not be where I am today.

Ed Powers

I am privileged to have had the opportunity to learn from your example. You were a role model for me in my early days in consulting, and I continue to be amazed by your accomplishments.

Rick Askew

I am eternally grateful to you for teaching me the critical role character, competence, and commitment play in one's success as a professional, especially when the stakes are high.

Alex Coassin

I cannot thank you enough for being the voice of wisdom and helping me recognize some of the greatest opportunities in my career. I am fortunate to have you as a friend.

Aaron Martinez

My dear friend and colleague, thank you for being my guide and role model as I navigated the firm. Without your guidance, I would not have been in a position to write this book.

Scott Day

My dear friend, your rock-solid support was instrumental to the completion of this book. I am forever in your debt.

Robert Sanders

My eternal gratitude to you, my friend, for your review of my manuscript and your brilliant ideas for improving it. Your frank feedback and intelligent questions made this a far better book than I had hoped for.

George Smolinski

Your help was crucial to getting this book ready for publishing, and I am tremendously thankful for your alacrity.

Jason P. Jordan

I am eternally grateful for your advice and encouragement during the early stages of my book project. You are a constant source of hope and inspiration.

Diana Navarro

My soulmate, throughout the project, no one was more on my side than you. You lived every word and every revision with me. This book would simply not exist, were it not for your sound counsel, patience, and encouragement. I feel blessed to have you in my life.

INTRODUCTION

What separates the highly successful consultants and firms from those that struggle to grow or fail outright?

At the risk of sounding obvious, your level of success (and that of your consulting firm) hinges first and foremost on your ability to find highly qualified clients to serve. In fact, this is the most critical function in any consulting firm. Finding highly qualified clients to serve is as important to your consulting firm as the air that you breathe is to your personal survival.

Then why do so many consultants rely on unpredictable, unreliable, and uncontrollable methods such as traditional "networking," content marketing, and social media campaigns to find highly qualified clients? Why leave anything to chance when there is an alternative that can guarantee with 100% certainty that you would reach a highly qualified client whenever you needed to?

I wrote this book to share that alternative with you. The system, strategies, and principles that I outline in this book will help you to find a nearly unlimited supply of high-quality, prospective clients, regardless of your industry or area of practice. They will help you to gain a significant advantage over your competition by beginning your interactions with those clients from a position of positive impact, implicit trust, and perceived competence.

When I began consulting in 1996, I knew very little about finding, reaching, and connecting with prospective clients. Over the many years of consulting with Ernst & Young (EY) and Deloitte, the largest professional services firms in the world at the time, I learned a number of strategies and techniques that those firms employed to find clients. But it was not until 2002, when I left Deloitte and started my own boutique consulting firm that I had to find my own clients. My experiences, triumphs, and failures were the genesis of the system outlined in this book.

Over the years, I improved, advanced, and updated that system with new techniques and strategies as I grew my consulting practice into a national concern. In 2011, when I took charge of building a new consulting practice for PricewaterhouseCoopers (PwC) in Seattle, I consolidated all the techniques and strategies into the system that you will learn in this book.

Who Should Read This Book?

Although the principles, strategies, and ideas in this book can be effective in many industries and professions, they have been proven time and again in the consulting industry. They are most helpful to consulting firm leaders and consultants with business development responsibilities who are looking for ways to grow their small or mid-size consulting firms and to develop predictable and reliable sources of leads and prospective clients.

The systems outlined in this book are designed to help any consulting professional find, reach, and connect with highly qualified clients, as long as those clients consist of other business professionals (in other words, not the general public or end consumers). Examples of consultants who should read this book include architectural consultants, marketing consultants, engineering consultants, business consultants, management consultants, and financial consultants.

What Makes This Book Unique?

This book offers a unique and contrarian approach to finding highly qualified consulting clients. While the majority of recent books published on this topic seem to promote new marketing strategies such as social media campaigns, content marketing, and online lead generation, this book teaches you how to find highly qualified consulting clients *without* relying on any of those strategies.

Admittedly, social media campaigns, content marketing, and online lead generation do have merit and will produce some results in most cases. However, they cannot produce predictable access to highly qualified clients in a reliable, repeatable, and controllable way. The systems, strategies, and principles in this book, on the other hand, provide you with a proven, predictable, and controllable means for finding highly qualified clients, regardless of the type of consulting that you engage in.

There are three important benefits you will gain from reading this book:

1. You will learn about the *Three Core Qualifications*™ that you (and everyone in your consulting firm) must demonstrate to your prospects and clients at all times to win their business and to keep them as clients for life. The failure to demonstrate these qualifications will likely result in your chasing the next client in short order.

2. You will learn a simple five-step system for finding highly qualified clients quickly, efficiently, and with minimal effort. Follow the step-by-step instructions to unlock a nearly unlimited supply of high-quality, prospective clients, regardless of your industry or area of practice.
3. You will learn how to maintain and improve the skills you learn from reading this book. As you become more efficient in implementing the systems, you will find new clients more quickly and with less effort.

Depending on how much time and effort you dedicate to implementing the strategies in this book, it is not uncommon to find, reach, and connect with your next, highly qualified client within 15 days of putting the system described here into practice.

I have used the same system I outline in this book time and time again to find consulting clients. In fact, I used this system to find, reach, and connect with my very first consulting client within a week of starting my boutique consulting firm. Even as a busy professional with firm leadership, client service, and operational responsibilities, the system outlined in this book should lead you to find your next highly qualified client within 30 days of putting the system into practice.

How to Use This Book

This book is like an hourglass: broad in focus in Parts One and Three, but tightly focused in Part Two. Part One provides you with the foundational knowledge that you need to ensure your success in implementing the system outlined in Part Two. Part Two provides you with a five-step system for finding, reaching, and connecting with highly qualified clients. Part Three builds on Parts One and Two to help you become more effective and efficient in implementing the system, strategies, and principles outlined in this book.

The chapters in Part One will help you to learn five reasons why many consultants fail in their efforts to find, reach, and win highly qualified clients. You will also discover the *Three Core Qualifications* that you must demonstrate to your prospects and clients at all times in order to win their business and keep them as clients for life.

The knowledge contained in these chapters is the necessary foundation you need to ensure your success when implementing the system outlined in this book.

The chapters in Part Two outline *The Client Catalyst System*™, a proven five-step system that is quite possibly the fastest, easiest, and most effective way to find highly qualified clients. Its unique approach requires no social media campaigns, no content marketing, and no online lead generation. It is a reliable, predictable, and repeatable system for finding, reaching, and connecting with consulting clients in any industry.

The chapters in Part Three help you to apply, improve, and update the skills that you have learned in this book.

How to Read This Book

This book is designed to be an "easy read." It is designed to be an informative book that provides you with the *why* and the *what*; it is not intended to be a detailed *how-to* or *what-if* manual.

Rather than an encyclopedic reference manual, this book is designed for rapid learning and speed of implementation. My goal for you is to read this book in a few hours and gain a sufficient understanding of the key principles so that you can immediately begin to implement the system outlined here in your consulting firm.

Because this book lays out a proven system, you should read through and implement the principles in each part and its chapters in sequence. I suggest that you take the following actions:

1. Read through Part One carefully to set yourself up for success. This part contains prerequisite knowledge for all consultants, regardless of your level of experience with consulting.

2. Skim Part Two to gain an overview and an understanding of the overall process and progression of the main system outlined in the book. Doing so will ensure that you understand the steps and how they fit into the "big picture."
3. Read Part Three so that you understand what you need to do on an ongoing basis to get better at implementing the systems, principles, and ideas outlined in this book.
4. Revisit and study Part Two in much more detail, and implement each step in the five-step system outlined in that part in sequence.
5. Leverage and avail yourself of the online resources I have provided to help you save time and effort in implementing the systems, principles, and strategies in the book.

Online Resources

There are many opportunities for you to gain access to free templates, worksheets, and online resources that can help you to save time and effort in implementing the strategies contained in this book. These resources are available to you free of charge by visiting *NeverChaseClientsAgain.com/BookBonuses*. Take advantage of them.

I have also developed products and services to help you to execute and implement the strategies, ideas, and systems that you learn here in your consulting firm. Where applicable, I remind you of the products and services that can accelerate your success in finding highly qualified clients. For a summary of the online resources, products, and services mentioned in this book, please refer to Appendix A.

An Important Request

If you feel that any part of the book needs additional explanation, please send me an email at *feedback@NeverChaseClientsAgain.com* with your thoughts and a reference to the relevant pages. I will rectify the issues for release in the next revision of the book.

Thank you so much in advance for your help in improving this book.

Part One

Prepare for Success

In this part of the book, you will learn the foundational knowledge that you need to successfully use the system outlined in Part Two to find, reach, and connect with highly qualified clients.

In the first chapter, you will learn the story of two consultants who choose different paths to building and growing a consulting firm. Their story illustrates five mistakes that often lead to failure.

In Chapter Two, you will discover the Three Core Qualifications that you and everyone in your consulting firm must demonstrate to your prospects and clients to win their business and to keep them as clients for life.

CHAPTER ONE

WHY MANY CONSULTANTS FAIL

A few years after starting my consulting firm, I met two highly skilled consultants, Jeff and Mark, at a networking event. They both worked in the same Big Four consulting firm (today, the Big Four consulting and accounting firms are Deloitte, EY, KPMG, and PwC). Both left their firm at about the same time with visions of starting their own consulting practices. Over the years, I kept in touch with both Jeff and Mark, and I witnessed their different approaches to building and growing a consulting firm — and the vast difference in their results.

Jeff was a highly skilled technologist with a penchant for spotting industry trends, and a passion for staying on the bleeding edge of technology. He thrived on solving complex problems with creative solutions that used the latest technologies. Jeff and his firm leadership disagreed on the market viability and potential of a trending technology he found fascinating, so he left his firm to explore those trends on his own by starting a consulting firm.

Mark, a consummate client service manager in his firm, excelled at building consensus, developing client relationships, and delivering complex projects. Although he enjoyed his work, Mark fundamentally disagreed with his firm leaders' approach to selling consulting work.

He believed that selling consulting services that the firm had little to no expertise in delivering, only because there was an opportunity to provide that service and generate revenue, was not in the best interest of the client. In his view, selling work and then hastily assembling a team of junior consultants who had little to no experience in delivering that work would only benefit the firm at the expense of the client and the consulting team assigned to the project. So he decided to leave his firm and build a consulting firm that better reflected his personal beliefs.

Four years after they left their firm to start their own consulting practices, Jeff and Mark found themselves in vastly different circumstances. Jeff's small consulting practice had never grown beyond four consultants. Although his practice was technically profitable, he rarely served more than one client at a time, and constantly found himself searching for new clients to serve. Jeff often began his workdays at 5 a.m. and ended them at 10 p.m. The stress of running his consulting practice had taken its toll on his personal life as well. His health had deteriorated considerably, and his relationships with his wife and children were strained.

Mark's consulting firm, on the other hand, had grown steadily, and now employed ten consultants and served two to three clients at any given time. He enjoyed exceptional working relationships with his clients, the majority of whom had been his clients continuously for years. He was entertaining the idea of establishing offices in new markets and taking on additional partners to help him to accomplish that goal. Curiously, Mark's personal life had also improved along with the success of his consulting firm. He was able to take several family vacations each year, and had even found the time to write a book.

By all accounts, Mark and Jeff began their journeys from a similar point in their careers. They had learned the art and practice of consulting in the same Big Four consulting firm. They both began with a vision of building a successful, growing consulting firm. So why did they produce such starkly different results? More importantly, what lessons can you learn from their examples as you set out to find highly qualified clients to grow your own consulting firm?

Five Mistakes that Lead to Failure

In hindsight, Jeff's failure and Mark's success in building a thriving consulting firm may be attributable to a number of factors such as differences in their abilities to deliver client projects, to sell consulting services, and to manage the operations of a consulting firm. One of the core reasons for the stark difference in their results was how they approached finding, reaching, and working with prospective clients.

In fact, Jeff committed no less than five mistakes that had ultimately led to his failure to grow a consulting firm. As we review each mistake and identify the key take-aways, ask yourself how you can learn from Jeff's mistakes to succeed in finding highly qualified clients to grow your consulting firm.

1. Prioritizing Digital Networking

In his haste to remain at the cutting edge of technology, Jeff invested time and resources in leveraging the latest social media platforms and online lead generation techniques to attract new clients. Mark, on the other hand, focused primarily on building personal relationships and secondarily on extending the reach of his professional network in established social media communities such as LinkedIn.

Whereas Jeff focused primarily on *digital* networking and relationship-building, Mark invested his time and energy primarily in *analog* networking — building personal relationships one person at a time — and leveraged his analog network to extend the reach of his *digital* network.

Although Jeff's network of loose connections spread far and wide across the latest social media communities, very few of those connections ever produced relevant leads or access to prospective clients. Jeff's knowledge of his social media connections was limited to the publicly-available information that they shared on each social media network. As you will learn in Chapters Five and Six, this shortcoming all but prevented Jeff from leveraging his connections to find, reach, and connect with highly qualified clients.

Mark's focus on analog networking, on the other hand, provided him with a personal knowledge and understanding of the goals, problems, and passions of his most valuable connections — including his current and past clients.

Mark's success in leveraging his analog network to find, reach, and connect with highly qualified prospects is a great testament to the belief that you do not need a digital network of 50,000 "friends," "connections," or "followers" to build a successful consulting firm. An analog network of a few valuable connections can be much more powerful than a vast digital network, as long as you possess a personal relationship with each connection.

Consulting has always been, and will always remain, a business that is built on personal (analog) relationships. In Part Two, we will discuss how to harness the true power of your analog network to find highly qualified clients to grow your consulting firm.

2. Investing in Ineffective, Unproven, and Unpredictable Means of Finding Clients

In addition to his investments of time and resources in leveraging the latest social media platforms and online lead generation techniques, Jeff also focused on content marketing to attract new clients. Although these strategies produced leads, the results were neither predictable nor repeatable. Very few of those leads were in fact highly qualified prospects in need of Jeff's services. With the additional time Jeff required to evaluate each lead, his return on his investment in these strategies was quite low.

When Jeff's content marketing and social media activities did result in inquiries from prospects, he often discovered that he possessed no advantage over his competitors in the eyes of those prospects. He often found himself participating in "beauty parades" and mired in Request For Proposal (RFP) processes.

The net result was that Jeff had very little time left to dedicate to other important activities and considerations that were needed to grow his consulting firm.

Mark, on the other hand, was able to leverage his relationships in his analog network to not only identify prospective clients, but to also connect with them through a mutually trusted colleague. By focusing his time and effort on methods that have been proven effective in finding prospective clients, Mark was rarely forced to participate in beauty parades and RFP processes. As a result, he had more time to dedicate to growing his consulting firm.

Clearly, one of the most critical choices you must make as a consultant and firm leader is deciding when, where, and how to spend your scarcest resource — your time. Investing time and energy in lead generation techniques that are inefficient or unpredictable will prevent you from allocating time to more effective techniques, which will inevitably lead to failure.

Many consultants and firm leaders are preoccupied with the question "How do we leverage social media and online lead generation techniques to find, attract, and win consulting clients?" A better question to ask is "What are the *most effective* ways to find, attract, and win consulting clients, and how can those ways be *enhanced* with social media and online lead generation techniques?"

The simple, five-step system you will learn in Part Two is quite possibly the most effective way to find, attract, and win consulting clients. This system does not require the use of social media campaigns and online lead generation techniques, but they can serve to enhance your results.

Free Online Resources

To evaluate the efficiency and effectiveness of your current lead generation techniques and to focus your time and efforts on those techniques that provide you with the highest returns, download a complementary *Lead Generation Evaluation Worksheet* by visiting *NeverChaseClientsAgain.com/LeadGenEval*.

3. Chasing the Wrong Clients

When Mark left his firm to start a consulting firm, his business strategy included a deliberate focus on providing only those services that he excelled in delivering. As his analog network grew, Mark's connections presented him with many opportunities, some of which did not align well with the services in his business strategy. Rather than dilute his focus, Mark remained committed to his chosen services, and did not pursue or take on clients with needs that were vastly different from those services.

Jeff, on the other hand, was spurred on to generate revenue because of his lack of progress in finding highly qualified clients. As a result, he was often forced to take on any client with a need that he could fulfill and the budget to pay for his services. By investing in ineffective, unproven, and unpredictable means of finding clients, Jeff had painted himself into a corner, forced to pursue *paying* clients over the *right* clients.

As a result, the majority of Jeff's clients were not only ill-qualified for the types of services he envisioned delivering when he started his consulting firm, they were often difficult to work with as individuals. He often found himself distracted by the friction between his consultants and his client's staff. He struggled with clients who insisted on micromanaging every aspect of the engagement. Many of his clients delegated projects to subordinates who were not in a position to affect change in the organization, in turn dooming the project to failure. Naturally, once he had delivered the services he had committed to with those clients, he would quickly move on to find the next — and hopefully better — client.

Many consulting firm leaders are concerned with the question "Where do we find clients we can serve?" A better question to consider is "What types of consulting clients should we be searching for?" To avoid repeating Jeff's mistakes, you must be able to answer both questions clearly, definitively, and directly.

4. Missing a Clear Definition of "Highly Qualified"

For Jeff's consulting practice, a highly qualified client was one with a need that his practice could serve and a budget to pay for those services. Because of the reasons discussed earlier, Jeff's primary motivation and sole criterion for selecting clients was generating revenue to keep the practice viable.

As a result, Jeff was forced to repeatedly refocus his consulting staff on solving disparate problems. This not only made it exceptionally difficult to provide the appropriate training to his staff consultants, it also prevented them from gaining any significant expertise and depth of knowledge in their specialization. Lack of professional growth, continuous shifts in focus, and lack of relevant training resulted in exceptionally high turnover rates among Jeff's consulting staff.

In contrast, Mark had a clear vision for the types of clients that his firm would pursue and accept. He defined a "highly qualified" client (or prospect) as one that met the following three conditions:

1. *Needs Alignment:* Present needs that were well-aligned with the firm's strategy and focus as well as with the skills and expertise of the firm's consulting staff.
2. *Client Fit:* Share the firm's work ethics and engagement style, have the financial means to pay the resulting consulting fees, and be in a position of authority to ensure the success of the project.
3. *Timing:* Require urgent assistance to fulfill their needs within 90 days. Prospects and clients whose needs were not urgent but met the other two conditions were considered "qualified," and pursued with less vigor than those who were considered "highly qualified."

Although Mark's definition is a great starting point, it is by no means complete. We will discuss the seven criteria that you should include in your definition of "highly qualified" in Chapter Three.

Nevertheless, because Mark's firm had a clear definition for who they considered "highly qualified" prospects and clients, and more importantly, remained committed to prioritizing clients who met that definition, Mark's firm gained many advantages over Jeff's consulting practice.

Mark and his firm developed strong personal and professional relationships with each and every client that they engaged, partially because they shared similar work ethics and working styles. With improved client relationships, Mark's firm was able to expand its reach across each client's organization and offer additional consulting services to fill its client's needs. Mark's team was well-suited to solve each client's problems, and in return, gained valuable experience and subject-matter expertise in its areas of specialization. Mark's firm developed and deepened its intellectual properties (IP) in its service areas, and gained industry recognition for its advancements.

Ideally, your firm's strategy should provide a clear definition for what you consider "highly qualified" prospects and clients. It should enable you to answer the questions "What types of clients will we pursue with vigor?" and "What types of consulting clients and engagements will we refuse?"

5. Ignoring What Clients Look For

During his employment with his former Big Four consulting firm, Mark had noticed that his clients often gravitated towards certain members of his team. The clients seemed more at ease with those individuals, expressed their feelings and concerns more readily to them, and requested them for critical tasks.

Upon discussing this observation with his clients, Mark had learned that those individuals demonstrated certain character traits and behaviors that his clients found invaluable. Those individuals:

- Appeared authentic, sincere, and candid, especially when interacting with their clients.
- Remained clear about their personal values and beliefs, and demonstrated a consistent congruity with those values, regardless of circumstances.
- Maintained a likable, friendly and approachable demeanor, especially when interacting with their client's staff.
- Demonstrated an interest in their client's business and a consistent commitment to their client's success.
- Provided insightful feedback and suggestions to their clients.
- Exhibited high levels of technical competence.
- Managed and met their client's expectations.

When Mark started his consulting firm, he infused these characteristics and behaviors into the culture and daily practices of his firm. As a result, he and his consulting teams developed stronger personal and professional relationships with their clients and their clients' staff, client engagements became easier to manage and complete, and Mark's firm was able to expand its reach across their clients' organizations with greater ease.

Jeff's consulting practice, on the other hand, never recognized what clients find invaluable or essential when choosing to retain a service provider. As a result, his practice never benefited from having a purposeful culture that advocated certain characteristics and behaviors. Combined with the other challenges mentioned above, Jeff's practice continued to struggle as it chased one client after another.

Many consulting firm leaders retrace their steps and examine their actions and approach when they fail to win client engagements. However, very few ever pause to evaluate their successes to discover why their clients chose them, and what critical factors, characters, and behaviors convinced their clients of the merits of the consulting firm and its team.

Understanding how and why we win clients is just as important, if not more so, than understanding the reasons why we lose them. This understanding is often the critical knowledge that separates those who succeed in consulting from those who fail. In the next chapter, we discuss this critical knowledge and what you must demonstrate to your prospects and clients to win their business and keep them as clients for life.

Summary

- There are five common mistakes that many consultants and consulting firms make, which often lead to failure: (1) Prioritizing digital networks, (2) Investing in ineffective, unproven, and unpredictable means of finding clients, (3) Chasing the wrong clients, (4) Missing a clear definition of "high quality", and (5) Ignoring what clients look for.
- An analog network of a few valuable connections can be much more powerful than a vast digital network, as long as you possess a personal relationship with each connection.
- Consulting has always been, and will always remain, a business that is built on personal (analog) relationships.
- To evaluate the efficiency and effectiveness of your current lead generation techniques and to focus your time and efforts on those techniques that provide you with the highest returns, download a complementary *Lead Generation Evaluation Worksheet* by visiting *NeverChaseClientsAgain.com/LeadGenEval*.
- Many firm leaders are preoccupied with the question "How do we leverage social media and online lead generation techniques to find, attract, and win consulting clients?" A

better question to ask is "What are the *most effective* ways to find, attract, and win consulting clients, and how can those ways be *enhanced* with social media and online lead generation techniques?"
- Many firm leaders are concerned with the question "Where do we find clients we can serve?" A better question to consider is "What types of consulting clients should we be searching for?" You must be able to answer both questions clearly, definitively, and directly.
- Having a clear definition for who you consider "highly qualified" prospects and clients, and more importantly, remaining committed to prioritizing clients who meet that definition, can provide you with many advantages over your competitors.
- Understanding how and why we win clients is just as important, if not more so, than understanding the reasons why we lose them. This understanding is often the critical knowledge that separates those who succeed in consulting from those who fail.

CHAPTER TWO

THREE CORE QUALIFICATIONS

How do clients choose between two consulting firms who possess the same levels of technical competence, similar market reputations, and comparable track records for successfully delivering client engagements?

This is a not a trivial question. In fact, many of your prospective and existing clients face this question every day. Their answer will determine whether they choose you over your competitors, both before they award a project, and afterwards, when your competitors work hard to replace you and your firm.

When your prospective clients choose you and your firm over your competitors, they are in effect risking their personal and professional reputation, their chances for career advancement, and quite possibly their livelihood. For your prospects and clients, choosing a consulting firm is never just a *business* decision; it is always a *personal* decision as well. Despite your best efforts to

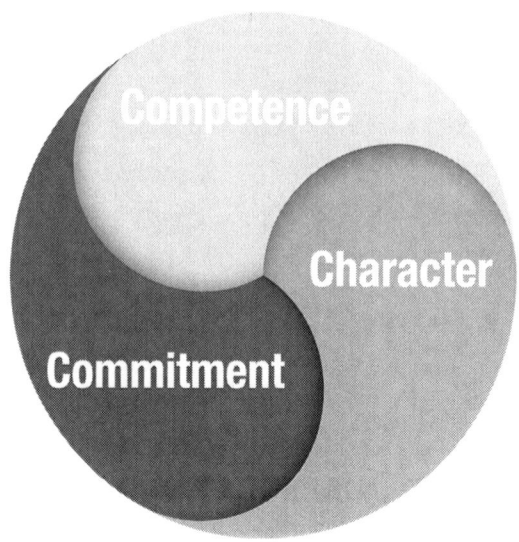

focus your prospects' and clients' attention on your professional competence, it is often your personal character and commitment that matter more to them.

Character, commitment, and competence are not qualifications that you can merely *assert*; you must *demonstrate* them from the moment of your first contact with your prospective client until the end of your mutual association.

Demonstrating the *Three Core Qualifications* of character, commitment, and competence builds the trust, authority, and credibility that earn you the right to serve your clients. It is the linchpin to growing your personal and professional relationships with your clients. It is the "X-factor" that leads a prospective client to choose you and your firm over your competitors time and time again.

When you, your team, or your firm fails to demonstrate your character, commitment, and competence, you can expect to lose prospective clients to competitors and to encounter resistance with existing clients. For example, failing to demonstrate the *Three Core Qualifications* can lead to:

- Prospects refusing to meet with you, postponing meetings repeatedly, or delaying decisions about hiring you and your firm.
- Prospects displaying minimal engagement and motivation during exploratory discussions.
- Prospects forcing you and your firm to compete for new work through "beauty contests" or other proposal activities.
- Clients or their staff mistreating, ignoring, or discounting your consulting team's efforts.
- Clients holding back on revealing their true goals, concerns, and new opportunities.
- Clients holding back on not making introductions to other prospects in their organizations.
- Clients delaying or refusing to give referrals inside or outside their organizations.
- Clients appearing demanding, micromanaging, or not involved.
- Clients challenging or refusing to pay your expenses or fees.
- Clients conducting a microscopic examination of your invoices and bills.
- Clients perceiving your deliverables as low quality, insufficient, or unimpressive.
- Client refusing to award follow-on work to you and your firm.

Recall our story of Jeff and Mark from the last chapter. Clearly, Jeff experienced a number of these challenges, whereas Mark did not. The consequences of not demonstrating the *Three Core*

Qualifications can be frustrating, wasteful, and costly, as you observed in Jeff's case.

We discuss how you can demonstrate your character, commitment, and competence to your prospects and clients in the sections that follow.

Demonstrating Your Character

Would you ever hire an unscrupulous accountant to manage your consulting firm's finances? What if that accountant was highly skilled, and had relevant experience working with professional services firms? What if that accountant also charged much lower fees than a comparable professional of good character? Chances are that you would choose not to hire an unscrupulous professional, regardless of any expertise or cost considerations.

The same is true for your prospects and clients. All else being equal, they prefer to work with professionals of good character over those with questionable character. In fact, they often prefer to work with professionals of good character *despite* possible disadvantages such as higher costs.

It is often difficult to describe what constitutes "good" character. We often judge good character based on *feelings* rather than logical reasoning, subjectively rather than objectively. There are no checklists or rational rules that those with good character follow. There are, however, common behaviors and actions that we associate with one or more character traits. These common behaviors and actions *demonstrate* or provide evidence for the character traits that we associate with them. For instance, we associate a steadfast adherence to one's principles when faced with adversity and challenges as a sign of integrity.

It is important to note that we make these associations between actions and character traits for both individuals and organization, such as companies and consulting firms. In fact, the character traits we associate with entities are often based on the behaviors and actions that we have observed from the individuals who represent those entities.

As a firm leaders, you must recognize the impact of your consulting staff's behaviors and actions in demonstrating your firm's character to your prospective and existing clients. One definitive way to ensure that your consulting staff demonstrate those character traits that you want your clients to attribute to your firm is to train your staff on the behaviors and actions that are often associated with each character trait.

The world's leading consulting firms such as Deloitte, EY, and PwC, recognize the importance of such training. They often require every new member of their consulting staff to complete training programs that instruct them on the acceptable behaviors and preferred actions that demonstrate the character traits that each firm considers a part of its brand.

Of the myriad character traits that you and your firm may consider a part of your brand, there are *Five Critical Character Traits™* that you and everyone in your firm must consistently demonstrate to win clients and to keep them for life.

Five Critical Character Traits

There are many character traits that can contribute to your success as a consultant. However, there are five that are absolutely critical to your ability to establish your credibility and build trust with your prospects and clients. They are:

1. Authenticity
2. Integrity

3. Empathy
4. Enthusiasm
5. Likability

We discuss each character trait in more detail in the sections that follow.

Authenticity

The majority of people define authenticity in the same way that the Merriam Webster Dictionary defines it: as the quality of being real and not false. They consider authenticity a function of presenting to others their true nature, beliefs, and values without deception, in other words, an *external* representation of who they are and what they stand for.

Authenticity with respect to your prospects and clients must go one step further to include both the *external* and the *internal* representations of who you are and what you stand for. You demonstrate authenticity when you are honest regarding your true knowledge, abilities, and values with your prospects and clients — *and* with yourself.

Ed Wallace, the author of *"Business Relationships That Last,"* defines authenticity as follows: "Authenticity is about being honest with ourselves and our clients regarding who we are and what we know; it is the quality of being genuine."

The principles of authenticity apply equally to you and your firm. There is no authenticity when you or your firm misrepresents yourself. Your prospects and clients will *sense* your lack of congruity in the moment, which will lead them to subconsciously doubt your character. Recall our discussion about how we often judge good character subjectively and based on feelings, rather than logical reasoning. In addition, when they eventually discover the truth, you will lose all credibility and trust.

An examination of Jeff's and Mark's differing approaches from the previous chapter reveals that Mark demonstrated his authenticity by pursuing and serving only those prospective clients who shared his firm's work ethics and engagement style, and who exhibited needs that were well-aligned with the services that Mark's firm excelled at delivering. Jeff, on the other hand, demonstrated a lack of authenticity by serving any client with the ability to pay Jeff's consulting fees, regardless of the type of work or his consulting team's expertise in delivering the services that the client required.

In order to gauge how well you and your firm demonstrate your authenticity, consider the following questions:

- Do you or your firm ever exaggerate your expertise, knowledge, or capabilities?
- Are your internal beliefs about your values, knowledge, and expertise congruent with those you project externally to your prospects and clients?
- Does everyone in your firm present the same level of authenticity to your prospects and clients in every interaction?
- How does each member of you consulting staff demonstrate this character trait to your prospects and clients?

True authenticity requires bravery, because you must be willing to represent yourself as you are. This may be very difficult at times, especially when the prospect's or client's perception of your image is important. But without authenticity, there is no credibility or trust.

Integrity

Integrity is the quality of adhering firmly and consistently to your chosen moral, ethical, or personal values. You demonstrate integrity when you stand publicly, openly, and unwaveringly for a specific set of values you have chosen to adopt.

Your integrity is the foundation of your credibility and trustworthiness. It leads your prospects and clients to believe that you will act predictably, morally, and ethically. They will judge your integrity based on how consistently your actions align with your assertions.

The key to demonstrating integrity is setting and meeting *expectations*. You must first set the expectations of your prospects and clients by declaring, asserting, or demonstrating your values or commitments. You must then act consistently and congruently with what you have declared, asserted, or demonstrated.

For instance, if you or your firm declare your unwavering commitment to acting in your clients' best interest, you must uphold that commitment in *everything* that you do: from emails, telephone conversations, and meetings prior to winning an engagement, to discussions and negotiations during the sales process, to collaboration and development of engagement deliverables. Your actions must remain aligned with your declared commitment consistently, or you risk tarnishing your integrity in the eyes of your prospects and clients.

As we saw in the previous chapter, Mark demonstrated his integrity by leaving his former consulting firm because that firm's approach to selling and delivering consulting work conflicted with his personal and professional values.

In order to gauge how well you and your firm demonstrate your integrity, consider the following questions:

- Are you crystal clear on your own values, commitments, and assertions, and are they crystal clear to your prospects and clients?
- Do you and everyone in your firm have a clear grasp of your values, commitments, and assertions that you have made to your prospects and clients?
- Are you aware of the personal values of each member of your consulting staff? If so, are they in agreement with the values of your firm and consulting practice?
- Do you have a clear grasp on the commitments and assertions your consulting staff have made (both implicitly and explicitly) to your prospects and clients, so that you can meet the resulting expectations?

If your values, commitments, and assertions are not crystal clear to you, they will not be crystal clear to your prospects and clients either. Ambiguity opens the door to interpretation, and your prospects and clients will define their expectations based on *their* values, which you do not control.

Empathy

Empathy is the quality of understanding others, sensing their feelings, and recognizing their motivations. You demonstrate empathy when you:

- Listen proactively to your prospects and clients with the intention of understanding them.
- Take conscious note of their emotional states.
- Work intently to understand their motivations.
- Reflect your appreciation of their intentions, feelings, and motivations in your words and actions.

As we learned earlier, choosing a consulting firm is never just a business decision; it is always a personal decision as well. Your prospects and clients will naturally prefer to work with someone who understands and appreciates them, both personally and professionally. The more clearly and consistently they can sense your empathy, the more likely it is that they will feel that you understand and appreciate them, and the more likely they will be to prefer you over your competitors.

One of the simplest ways to demonstrate your empathy is to understand and behave in accordance with your prospect's and client's *Behavioral Style*. Behavioral Styles classify an individual's inherent communication, motivation, and learning preferences into categories, or "styles." When you understand your clients' Behavioral Styles, you can predict how they think, feel, and perceive the world around them. It enables you to communicate with them more effectively, influence them more readily, and relate to them more perceptively.

There are several scientifically designed and validated methods for identifying an individual's Behavioral Styles. One of the simplest and most effective methods is the *DISC Behavioral Styles*. Since a thorough discussion of this method is beyond the scope of this book, I highly recommend that you prioritize learning this method to help you relate more powerfully to your clients.

Empathy is the key that unlocks the door to stronger client relationships. Learning to use Behavioral Styles is akin to having a master key.

In order to evaluate how well you and your firm demonstrate your empathy for your prospects and clients, consider the following questions:

- How perceptive are you about your prospect's and client's intentions, feelings, and motivations?
- How well do you understand their Behavioral Styles?
- How proactively do you seek to understand and appreciate them, and how consistently do you reflect your appreciation in your actions?
- What means or mechanisms does your firm employ to gain a better understanding of your prospect's and client's intentions, feelings, and motivations?
- How well does each member of your consulting staff perform in this area?

Enthusiasm

Enthusiasm is a willingness and cheerful readiness to do something. It is one of the most powerful character traits that a consultant can cultivate. When your team and colleagues observe your readiness and willingness to take action, to tackle challenges head-on, and to maintain a positive attitude, they will be motivated to work harder as well.

When your prospects and clients perceive you as ready and willing to assist them, they begin to trust you. Your willingness and readiness to act in the face of challenges signals your confidence, which most people subconsciously associate with your competence and commitment. This, in turn, increases their perception of your credibility and trustworthiness.

Professionals who possess enthusiasm often demonstrate the following behaviors and actions:

- They are passionate about what they do, their firms, and their clients.
- They always look for and highlight the positives in any situation.

- They maintain a high level of energy when pursuing their goals.
- They are eager to tackle challenges head-on.
- They are rarely discouraged, and always see opportunities where others see failure.

Considering the experiences of Jeff and Mark from the previous chapter, Jeff's passion for staying on the cutting edge of technology helped him to demonstrate enthusiasm when the opportunity presented itself. However, Jeff rarely had the opportunity to exercise his passion due to poor choices that prevented him from pursuing client projects that involved cutting edge technologies.

What are some of the other behaviors and actions that you have observed in others who exhibit the character trait of enthusiasm? What behaviors and actions do you believe are critical for you to demonstrate to develop this character trait in yourself?

True enthusiasm is highly contagious. Cultivate it in yourself, and you will have the power to influence and motivate others to follow you.

Likability

Likability is the quality of being agreeable, approachable, and friendly. It is what leads others to enjoy your company and influences them to want to associate with you. Your likability is based on what others perceive about your intentions, as well as the results of your actions.

For instance, your prospects and clients will perceive you as more likable when they recognize your intentions to add value to their lives and be helpful in any way you can. They will also perceive you as likable when your actions benefit them directly or indirectly.

As we learned earlier, choosing a consulting firm is never just a business decision for your prospects and clients; it is always a personal decision as well. All else being equal, they will prefer to work with those consultants and firms who they find more likable. In fact, many prospects will choose to avoid consultants who they do not find likable, therefore minimizing the possibility of awarding any work to those consultants.

How likable do your prospects and clients find you, your consulting team, and your firm? How have you determined your likability from *their* viewpoints? What actions and behaviors do you believe will make you and your firm more likable?

Demonstrating Your Commitment

Have you ever been contacted by a stranger who "pitched" his products to you, asked you for a favor, or requested your help without offering anything of value in exchange? If so, did you oblige him?

If you are like most people, chances are that you refused that person's request the moment you realized that the *intent* of his request was not to provide a mutual benefit or to compensate you in exchange for your help. You refused that person's request when you recognized his selfish *intent* and his lack of *commitment* to providing you with anything of value.

When you approach your prospects and clients, they will feel the same way about *your* requests unless they perceive your intent to provide mutual benefit and recognize your *commitment* to adding value to their lives.

To demonstrate your commitment to your prospects and clients, you must therefore accomplish three outcomes:

1. Add value to their personal or professional lives.
2. Add this value *before* you request anything in exchange.

3. Ensure that what you request is either of far less value than the value you provided, or that it provides mutual value to you *and* your prospects and clients.

Think of this as making deposits into a bank account before making withdrawals. Under normal circumstances, you must make larger deposits than what you intend to withdraw.

Your success in adding value to your prospects and clients hinges on the accuracy of your answers to the following *Value Questions*:

- What do my prospects and clients find valuable?
- How do I provide them with what they find valuable?
- How do I verify that they indeed *perceived* value from what I provided them?

You may be in a position to answer the Value Questions with more accuracy with regards to your existing clients, especially if you have developed a close working relationship with them. However, you are far less likely to find accurate answers with regards to your prospects.

The ability to find accurate answers to the Value Questions is one of the key elements of the five-step system that you will learn in Part Two of this book. For a more detailed discussion and specific instructions on answering these questions, refer to Chapters Six and Seven.

Based on what we learned about the experiences of Jeff and Mark, can you guess how Mark demonstrated his commitment to his prospects and clients by adding value to their lives? If you recall, Mark focused primarily on analog networking, which provided him with personal knowledge and understanding of the goals, problems, and passions of his most valuable connections. Using this knowledge and the input from his network of personal relationships, Mark was able to answer the Value Questions with relative accuracy. All that remained was for him to take action on the Value Questions.

Can you answer the Value Questions accurately with regards to your existing clients? Can you answer them with regards to your prospects? If not, where can you find the information you need?

Demonstrating Your Competence

Of the Three Core Qualifications, competence is where the majority of consulting professionals focus their attention. After all, your prospective clients choose to hire you and your firm to solve a problem that requires professional competence and specialized knowledge in certain areas. To earn your prospect's and client's confidence, you must demonstrate your professional competence in those areas.

Generally speaking, professional competence can be attributed to your proficiency in three categories of skills that you must demonstrate to your prospects and clients. These skills categories are:

1. Hard Skills
2. Soft Skills
3. Consultative Skills

We discuss each category of skills in more detail in the sections that follow.

Hard Skills

Hard Skills refer to the types of knowledge and expertise that are technical, procedural, or functional in nature. They encompass subject matter expertise, product and industry knowledge, knowledge of regulatory procedures, and expertise related to processes and procedures.

The majority of professionals and consulting firms rely heavily on their Hard Skills to demonstrate their professional competence. However, Hard Skills are no longer sufficient to distinguish yourself among your competitors. Now more than ever, prospective clients have access to a tremendous pool of professionals and consulting firms with strong Hard Skills. Overemphasizing your skills in this area, especially at the expense of the other two skills categories, can diminish your prospective client's perception of your overall competence.

There are, however, exceptions to this observation. For instance, smaller firms that often compete with larger firms for highly technical client engagements can differentiate themselves by demonstrating extraordinarily strong Hard Skills. By positioning themselves as "specialty firms" with deep skills in a given technical area, smaller firms can successfully compete for client engagements where such skills are pivotal to the engagement's success.

Regardless of the size of your consulting firm, there are many options for you and your consulting staff to demonstrate your Hard Skills to your prospective clients. The following is a partial list to help you brainstorm potential options:

- Publish a research paper, white paper, or special report on the specific problems that your prospective clients face.
- Develop and publish a training program on your subject matter.
- Produce and publish a newsletter that outlines current trends in your prospective client's industry.
- Write and publish a book on the processes and procedures in your areas of expertise.

How much emphasis do you place on your Hard Skills, compared to the other two skills categories, when communicating with prospective clients? How do you demonstrate your Hard Skills today? In what additional ways can you demonstrate your Hard Skills in the specific areas that are relevant to the problems your prospective clients need you to solve?

Soft Skills

Soft Skills refer to your abilities to interact, collaborate, and work with other people. They encompass the "people skills" that are often associated with emotional intelligence. Solving client problems often requires you to cooperate, coordinate, and collaborate with people, all of which rely on your Soft Skills to succeed.

Strong Soft Skills are also essential to building better relationships with your prospects and clients. Recall our discussion about the Five Critical Character Traits earlier in this chapter. Strong Soft Skills signal a high degree of empathy, and they contribute to your likability.

Many technically gifted consultants lack strong Soft Skills and attempt to compensate for this shortcoming by over-emphasizing their Hard Skills. As we discussed in the previous section, strong Hard Skills cannot displace the need for strong Soft Skills; they are both necessary to demonstrate your overall professional competence.

By their very nature, Soft Skills are difficult to completely categorize and enumerate completely. However, there are *Seven Essential Soft Skills*™ that you should strive to demonstrate to your prospects and clients. These skills are:

1. Managing Expectations
2. Communicating Clearly

3. Understanding People
4. Seeking and Giving Feedback
5. Resolving Conflicts
6. Collaborating in a Team
7. Managing Your Emotional States

A detailed discussion of the Seven Essential Soft Skills is beyond the scope of this book. To learn more about these skills, to evaluate your proficiency (or that of your consulting staff), and to obtain additional resources and training programs related to these skills, please visit *NeverChaseClientsAgain.com/SoftSkills*.

How would you rate your proficiency in each of the Seven Essential Soft Skills? How would you rate your consulting staff's proficiency? How do your prospects and clients rate your proficiency, as well as the proficiency of your consulting staff?

Consultative Skills

Consultative Skills are the fusion of discrete abilities such as analytical thinking, problem solving, deductive and inferential reasoning, and root-cause analysis, among others, which enable you to effectively analyze and solve your clients' problems. In essence, Consultative Skills bridge your Hard Skills and Soft Skills to help you accomplish *The Five Ps of Consulting*:

- **Pinpoint** the problems that your clients need to solve.
- **Perform** the necessary work to devise a solution.
- **Produce** the solution into a set of deliverables.
- **Package** the deliverables for discussion, implementation, or communication.
- **Present** the packaged deliverables to the appropriate stakeholders.

Your prospects and clients will never perceive you as a competent consultant unless and until you can demonstrate your Consultative Skills by successfully engaging in and completing each of The Five Ps of Consulting. Clearly, you will be in a better position to do so with your existing clients than with potential prospects.

The ability to demonstrate your Consultative Skills to prospective clients is one of the key elements of the five-step system that you will learn in Part Two of this book. For a more detailed discussion and specific instructions on this topic, refer to Chapters 6 through 8.

By their very nature, these abilities and the Consultative Skills they produce cannot be learned by just reading about them; they must be practiced. The world's leading consulting firms such as Deloitte, EY, and PwC, recognize the importance of providing their consulting staff with opportunities to practice these skills in training environments that offer active feedback by an instructor. They often require every new member of their consulting staff to complete training programs that enhance their Soft Skills and Consultative Skills before participating in their first client assignments.

In order to assess the need for such training programs in your consulting firm, consider the following questions:

- How would you rate your proficiency in each of the Five Ps of Consulting?
- How would you rate your consulting staff's proficiency?
- How do your prospects and clients rate your proficiency, as well as the proficiency of your consulting staff?
- How do you ensure that your consulting staff possess and demonstrate consistently strong Consulting Skills to your clients?

Demonstrating the Three Core Qualifications

Demonstrating the Three Core Qualifications of character, commitment, and competence builds the trust, authority, and credibility that lead a prospective client to choose you and your firm over your competitors time and again.

All prospects and clients evaluate you and your firm based on how well you demonstrate these qualifications. This evaluation is often an *unconscious* activity, rather than a consciously planned and conducted assessment. To illustrate this fact, consider how you might label a professional who demonstrates only two of the Three Core Qualifications.

Failing your prospective client's unconscious evaluation may earn you and your firm one or more of the labels listed in the table on the following page.

Additionally, many of the common challenges in dealing with prospects and clients can be traced to a failure to demonstrate one or more of the Three Core Qualifications. You must therefore strive to demonstrate *all three* of the Core Qualifications whenever the opportunity presents itself.

It is important to note that your prospects and clients continuously evaluate each of your firm's consultants, and particularly your firm's leaders, on their ability to demonstrate the Three Core Qualifications. If your consulting team members or firm leaders lack proficiency in one or more of the Three Core Qualifications, you should consider providing them with additional training. For more information on proficiency evaluation and training resources, please visit *NeverChaseClientsAgain.com/CoreTraining*.

Your new, foundational understanding of the Three Core Qualifications will be essential to your success in finding, reaching, and connecting with highly qualified clients as you

Character	Commitment	Competence	How a Prospective Client Might Label You
X	✓	✓	unscrupulous, untrustworthy, unprincipled
✓	X	✓	selfish, inconsiderate, unreasonable
✓	✓	X	unqualified, unfit, unprepared

implement the five-step system I have outlined in Part Two of this book.

Summary

- For your prospects and clients, choosing a consulting firm is never just a *business* decision; it is always a *personal* decision as well.
- Despite your best efforts to focus your prospect's and client's attention on your professional competence, it is often your personal character and commitment that matters more to them.
- Demonstrating the *Three Core Qualifications* of character, commitment, and competence is the "X-factor" that leads a prospective client to choose you and your firm over your competitors time and time again. You must demonstrate them from the moment of your first contact with your prospective client until the end of your mutual association.
- There are *Five Critical Character Traits* that you and your firm must demonstrate consistently to win clients and keep

- them for life. They are: (1) Authenticity, (2) Integrity, (3) Empathy, (4) Enthusiasm, and (5) Likability.
- To demonstrate your commitment to your prospects and clients, you must accomplish three outcomes: (1) Add value to their personal or professional lives, (2) add this value *before* you request anything in exchange, and (3) ensure that what you request is either of far less value than the value you provided, or it provides mutual value to you *and* your prospects and clients.
- Professional competence can be attributed to your proficiency in three categories of skills that you must demonstrate to your prospects and clients. These skills categories are (1) Hard Skills, (2) Soft Skills, and (3) Consultative Skills.
- All prospects and clients evaluate you and your firm based on how well you demonstrate these qualifications. This evaluation is often an *unconscious* activity, rather than a consciously planned and conducted assessment.
- If your consulting team members or firm leaders lack proficiency in one or more of the Three Core Qualifications, you should consider providing them with additional training. For more information on proficiency evaluation and training resources, please visit *NeverChaseClientsAgain.com/CoreTraining*.

PART TWO

FIND HIGHLY QUALIFIED CLIENTS

In this part, you will learn a proven, five-step system for finding highly qualified clients in a reliable, predictable, and repeatable fashion.

Chapter Three provides an overview of the five steps in the system. Each of the succeeding chapters in this part outlines one step of the system in more detail.

CHAPTER THREE

THE CLIENT CATALYST SYSTEM

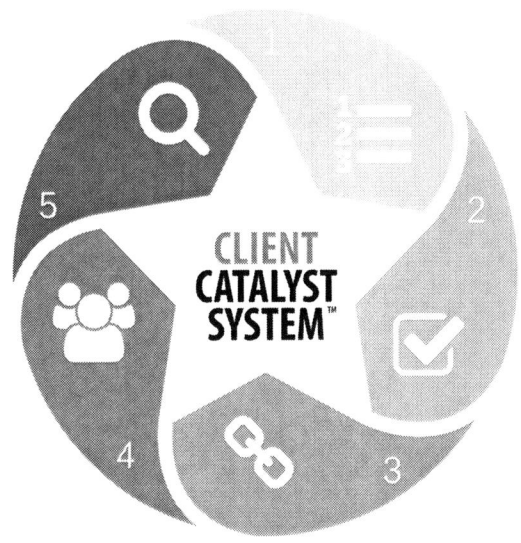

This chapter provides an overview of the *Client Catalyst System™*, a proven five-step system designed to help you find a nearly unlimited supply of high-quality, prospective clients, regardless of your industry or area of practice.

This unique system provides you with a significant advantage over your competition because, at its core, it is designed to help you demonstrate your proficiency in the Three Core Qualifications during your initial contact with those highly qualified prospective clients. As a result, you begin your interactions with those clients from a position of credibility, implicit trust, and perceived competence.

Overview and Summary

Expressed in its simplest form, this system can be depicted as shown below.

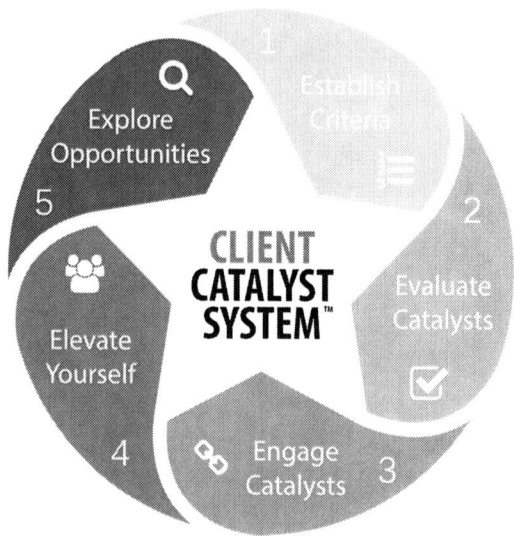

This chapter summarizes each of these steps, while the succeeding chapters explore each step in more detail. For a "quick reference" summary of the steps, please refer to Appendix B.

Step One: Establish Criteria

The main objective of this step is to develop a clear definition of whom you consider "highly qualified." As discussed earlier in Chapter One, the lack of this clear definition is one of the factors that could ultimately lead to failure.

In this step, you will:

1. Identify the specific criteria that a prospect must meet in order to be considered highly qualified
2. Verify that you can articulate the details of the criteria you identified in the previous step and create a list of potential prospects (individuals and organizations) that satisfy those criteria based on preliminary research

This step is discussed in detail in Chapter Four.

Step Two: Evaluate Catalysts

The main objective of this step is selecting a Catalyst with the right qualifications and characteristics to help you to reach your highly qualified clients. The term "Catalyst" refers to an individual who can facilitate access to others, without personally participating in the introduction process. For a more detailed definition, please refer to Chapter Five.

In this step, you will:

1. Discover the purpose of a Catalyst.
2. Learn the specific qualifications and characteristics that a Catalyst must possess.

3. Define a pool of potential Catalysts with access to your highly qualified clients.
4. Identify the top Catalysts you will engage in Step Three.

This step is discussed in detail in Chapter Five.

Step Three: Engage Catalysts

The main objective of this step is to motivate a potential Catalyst to facilitate your access to your highly qualified clients.

In this step, you will:

1. Determine what you can offer to your potential Catalyst to add value to his or her life.
2. Present your offering of value to your Catalyst in a way that motivates that person to help you.

This step is discussed in detail in Chapter Six.

Step Four: Elevate Yourself

The main objective of this step is to present your highly qualified clients with an offering that adds value to their lives and elevates you above your competition in their minds.

In this step, you will:

1. Seek the assistance of your Catalyst to identify an offering of exceptional value to your highly qualified clients.
2. Leverage your Catalyst's position to connect with your highly qualified clients.
3. Present your value offering in a way that demonstrates your proficiency in the Three Core Qualifications.

This step is discussed in detail in Chapter Seven.

Step Five: Explore Opportunities

The main objective of this step is to leverage the good will that you have cultivated with your highly qualified clients to identify and explore opportunities to serve them.

In this step, you will:

1. Identify opportunities to serve your highly qualified clients.
2. Determine if your highly qualified clients can help you reach other prospective clients.
3. Collaborate with your highly qualified clients to determine how you can serve them.

This step is discussed in detail in Chapter Eight.

Free Online Resources

As a reader of this book, you have access to additional resources such as checklists, templates, and worksheets to help you to save time and effort when implementing the Client Catalyst System. These resources are available to you online by visiting *NeverChaseClientsAgain.com/BookBonuses*.

For a summary of all online resources, products, and services mentioned in this book, please refer to Appendix A.

CHAPTER FOUR

STEP 1. ESTABLISH CRITERIA

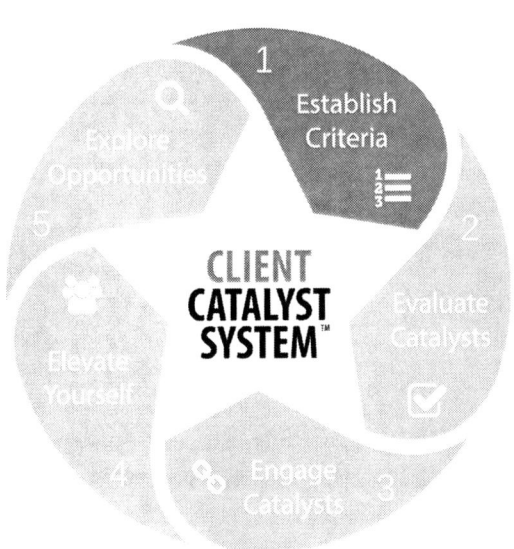

From our story about Jeff and Mark, we learned that to succeed you must remain committed to serving a group of highly qualified clients. We also learned that you must define with clarity the set of criteria that prospective clients must meet to be considered "highly qualified." Without this definition, you are likely to waste considerable time, effort, and resources on chasing the wrong clients.

In this chapter, you will learn how to implement the first step of the Client Catalyst System. In the sections that follow, you will define, verify, and commit to the criteria that will guide your client pursuits as you follow the remaining steps of the Client Catalyst System.

1.1 Identify Your PATRONS Criteria™

The first step in finding highly qualified prospective clients to pursue is to define the criteria that you will use to identify them. Use the following seven criteria as a starting point to define the specific criteria that work for you and your firm:

1. **P**urchasing Power
2. **A**uthority
3. **T**iming
4. **R**oles and Responsibilities
5. **O**rganization
6. **N**eeds
7. **S**tyle

Use the acronym PATRONS to remember these seven criteria. The following sections discuss each criterion in more detail.

Purchasing Power

Clearly, the number one factor that separates prospective clients from non-clients is their ability to pay your firm's consulting fees. What is the minimum purchasing power prospective clients must possess for you to consider them "highly qualified?"

Note that this criterion is not concerned with the overall fees associated with the smallest engagement you are willing to accept. Instead, this criterion specifies the minimum level of funds that prospective clients must have at their disposal to be considered "highly qualified." In all likelihood, highly qualified prospective clients will engage you for a small "trial" project before advancing to larger, more complex ones that carry higher fees. Therefore, the focus of this criterion is the prospective client's funding, not the size or fees associated with a potential engagement.

Authority

This criterion specifies the types or levels of authority prospective clients must possess to be considered "highly qualified." At a minimum, you should consider including two types of authority requirements in this criterion:

1. *Signing Authority:* Is it necessary for prospective clients to have the authority to sign contracts (i.e., enter their organizations into binding agreements) before you consider them highly qualified?
2. *Decision Authority:* What level of decision-making authority (e.g., decision makers, approvers, or users) must prospective clients possess before you consider them highly qualified?

Timing

Ideally, a highly qualified prospective client would have an urgent need for the services you provide. With this criterion, you specify the level of that urgency.

How soon must prospective clients require your services for you to consider them highly qualified? How quickly must they commit to or intend to begin a project or engagement?

Roles and Responsibilities

Your prospective client's position, title, and roles and responsibilities are often significant factors that contribute to the success or failure of a consulting engagement. When defining this criterion, consider your prospective client's position, title, roles, and responsibilities in his or her organization, as well as in the broader industry and market.

Organization

This criterion specifies the organizational factors that you consider significant when choosing to pursue a prospective client. These factors often affect a prospective client's purchasing power, authority, and timing. When considering this criterion, include factors such as an organization's:

- Type
- Size
- Revenue
- Customers
- Industry
- Geographic Area
- Market Segment

What are the organizational factors that must be present for you to consider a prospective client "highly qualified?"

Needs

Ideally, a highly qualified prospective client exhibits needs that align well with your firm's services, expertise, and strategic goals. However, it is often challenging to evaluate the hidden, internal needs and problems of a prospective client's organization, especially without *inside knowledge* of that organization. Therefore, when considering this criterion, focus on the *external* manifestations of your prospective client's needs and problems.

What external, visible characteristics or "symptoms" would a prospective client's organization exhibit that would signal a need or problem that your firm is well-positioned to solve?

Style

Although this factor is often ignored, a prospective client's work ethics and engagement management style can have a significant impact on a consulting engagement's success, as well as on the morale of the consulting team involved.

What are the ethical, managerial, and working style considerations that are important to you when choosing which prospective clients to pursue?

PATRONS Criteria in Action

When I took charge of building a new consulting practice at PwC in Seattle, my first priority was to identify the clients who I would actively pursue. Researching the pool of regional clients, I recognized that the client service directors and regional sales and marketing executives focused primarily on the well-known household brands in the region. This focus was not based on an assessment of any specific criteria, results of market research, or known client needs. Instead, this focus was based on the assumption that well-known brands were better positioned and more willing to buy consulting services.

I approached my client selection by defining my PATRONS Criteria. The following is a summary of my selections for each criterion:

- *Purchasing Power:* Highly qualified clients would have an annual consulting budget exceeding $1 million, ideally demonstrated by previous engagements with the Big Four consulting firms during the prior year.
- *Authority:* Highly qualified clients would have both signing authority and decision-making authority regarding the selection and engagement of a consulting firm.
- *Timing:* Highly qualified clients would be ready to begin a consulting engagement with the next 90 days.
- *Roles & Responsibilities:* Highly qualified clients would occupy the highest position in their given responsibility center. Titles that were relevant to my selection included Chief Technology Officer (CTO), Chief Security Officer (CSO), Chief Information Officer (CIO), or a Vice President with comparable responsibilities.
- *Organization:* Highly qualified clients would belong to a privately- or publicly-held organization in the Pacific Northwest region of the United States, with annual revenues exceeding $1 billion.
- *Needs:* Highly qualified clients would have (a) acquired another organization, (b) launched new technology platforms, divisions, or services, or (c) experienced public information security breaches during the prior calendar year.

- *Style:* Highly qualified clients would (a) view me and my firm as equals (not subordinates), (b) regard my consulting team as highly valuable members of their team, (c) show interest in developing our professional relationship, and (d) declare their intentions to take an active role in the management of the engagement, including the dedication of sufficient time and resources to facilitate the necessary work.

Developing these PATRONS Criteria was an essential step that helped me to eliminate a number of potential clients from consideration, and to avoid wasting time on several popular companies that were not likely to buy consulting services from my practice. Armed with these PATRONS Criteria, I was ready to begin the next step in the process.

Free Online Resources

To save time when defining your PATRONS Criteria and evaluating prospective clients on their qualifications compared to those criteria, download a complementary *Client Qualification Checklist* by visiting NeverChaseClientsAgain.com/ClientQualChecklist.

1.2 Verify Your Criteria

Once you have defined your PATRONS Criteria, the next step is to verify that you can articulate them clearly and that there are indeed individuals or organizations that meet those criteria. This is an important step for two reasons:

1. In Step Two of the Client Catalyst System, you will identify potential "Catalysts" who can facilitate your access to highly qualified prospective clients. Being able to articulate

your PATRONS Criteria and having a preliminary list of individuals or companies that meet those criteria will be an essential enabler in this step.
2. In Step Three of the Client Catalyst System, you will engage and motivate potential Catalysts to help you gain access to highly qualified prospective clients. The more clearly you can articulate your PATRONS Criteria to your Catalysts, the more likely they will be to successfully identify and facilitate that access.

The simplest way to verify your PATRONS Criteria is to conduct an Internet search for qualifying organizations and professionals. Bear in mind that your primary objective in this step is *not* to compile a complete list of prospective clients to pursue (as you would in traditional "prospecting"). Instead, your primary objective is to verify the existence of organizations and professionals that meet your PATRONS Criteria, so that you can better identify potential Catalysts who are knowledgeable about them and who can direct you to them.

Ideally, your search should identify a dozen or more specific organizations and professionals that meet the majority of your PATRONS Criteria.

1.2.1 Search for Organizations

Begin your Internet research on a search engine such as Google. Search for organizations that meet the Organization, Needs, and Purchasing Power criteria you defined in the previous step. Take note of number of results your search produces. Record the names and information associated with your criteria for a sampling of the resulting organizations.

1.2.2 Search for Professionals

Conduct an Internet and social media search for professionals who meet the Authority, Roles and Responsibilities, and Style criteria that you defined in the previous step. Begin your search with the sample organizations you identified during your previous search. Record the names and information associated with a sampling of the individuals who you identify in your search.

Free Online Resources

Modern search engines such as Google allow for the use of advanced "search strings" that can save you considerable time and effort when conducting an online search. To download a *Google Search Cheat Sheet* and sample advanced "search strings" to use in your online search, visit *NeverChaseClientsAgain.com/GoogleCheatSheet*.

1.3 Commit to Your PATRONS

Once you have defined and verified your PATRONS Criteria, you must commit consciously, deliberately, and publicly to pursuing *only* those highly qualified prospective clients that meet the majority of your criteria.

Without such a deliberate commitment, you are likely to waste considerable time, effort, and resources on chasing the wrong clients. In addition, you risk confusing your prospective clients, your consulting staff, and the general market about who you specialize in serving. This lack of commitment can lead to your failure in gaining traction in your marketplace.

Your best course of action is to commit your limited time, energy, and resources to your chosen client pursuit strategy:

pursue only those prospective clients who you have identified as "highly qualified," and consciously refuse to pursue other opportunities. As David Maister advises in his book "*Strategy And The Fat Smoker,*" "Strategy is deciding whose business you are going to turn away."

1.3.1 Make a Public Commitment

You should consider committing publicly to your strategy of pursuing *only* highly qualified prospective clients that meet the majority of your PATRONS Criteria. Such a public commitment can have powerful benefits:

- *It empowers others to refer prospective clients to you.* One of the reasons that your contacts may not refer others to you is their lack of understanding and clarity of exactly whom you serve and how those referrals benefit from your services. By publicly defining the target clients that you wish to serve, you provide much-needed clarity to those contacts who are in a position to refer prospective clients to you.
- *It enhances your position among your prospects, clients, and peers.* When you publicly commit to serving only a specific community of prospective clients, they begin to perceive you as a professional (or firm) who *specializes* in solving their specific problems. When faced with a choice to either hire a "generalist" firm or one that specializes in solving their particular problems (i.e., you), most prospective clients would choose the latter option.
- *It informs your consulting staff.* Many consulting firms suffer from a disconnect between the firm leadership and the consulting staff who engages clients on a daily basis. Consulting staff is often unaware of the strategic direction

that the firm's leaders have chosen to pursue. As the eyes and ears of your consulting firm, your staff members are well-positioned to identify new opportunities and to inform others in your client's organization about the services your firm offers. A well-informed staff can be a powerful "opportunity scout" and ambassador for you and your firm.
- *It differentiates you from others in your market.* The majority of consulting firms hope to differentiate themselves from others in their market through "quality of service" and "client orientation." Although these factors are important, they are not a prime differentiator because every firm in the market provides "quality of service" and "client orientation." These factors and others like them are a prerequisite for remaining in business. Market specialization, on the other hand, is a prime differentiator.

There are several options for committing publicly to your client pursuit strategy. The following is a partial list of actions that you can take to accomplish that goal:

- Post a short summary of your PATRONS Criteria on your firm's website.
- Write and publish a press release that outlines who your highly qualified prospective clients are and how you intend to serve them.
- Write a short sentence declaring who your highly qualified prospective clients are and include it in your firm's standard "email signature."
- Update your social media profiles with a clear summary of who your highly qualified prospective clients are and how you intend to serve them.

In the next chapter, you will use the information that you have compiled here to select a Catalyst with the right qualifications and characteristics to help you reach your highly qualified clients.

Summary

- To succeed, you must remain committed to serving only prospective clients that are "highly qualified."
- The first step in finding highly qualified prospective clients to pursue is to define the criteria you will use to identify them.
- The seven criteria you should consider defining to identify highly qualified clients are: (1) Purchasing Power, (2) Authority, (3) Timing, (4) Roles and Responsibilities, (5) Organization, (6) Needs, and (7) Style. Use the acronym PATRONS to remember these criteria.
- To save time when defining your PATRONS Criteria, download a complementary *Client Qualification Checklist* by visiting *NeverChaseClientsAgain.com/ClientQualChecklist*.
- Once you have defined your PATRONS Criteria, the next step is to verify that you can articulate them clearly and that there are indeed individuals or organizations that meet those criteria.
- The simplest way to verify your PATRONS Criteria is to conduct an Internet search for qualifying companies and professionals. Ideally, your search should identify a dozen or more specific organizations and professionals that meet the majority of your PATRONS Criteria.
- To download a *Google Search Cheat Sheet* and sample advanced "search strings" to use in your online search, visit *NeverChaseClientsAgain.com/GoogleCheatSheet*.

- To succeed, you must commit your limited time, energy, and resource to your chosen client pursuit strategy. A public commitment to your strategy can have powerful benefits.

CHAPTER FIVE

STEP 2. EVALUATE CATALYSTS

In the last chapter, you developed the criteria that you will use to identify highly qualified clients. Armed with that essential foundation, you are now ready to take the next step: to find individuals with the right qualifications and characteristics who can facilitate your access to those highly qualified clients. It is essential that you complete the work in the previous chapter before proceeding to locate and connect with a Catalyst. You must have a clearly-defined and verified set of criteria to identify the right Catalyst.

In this chapter, you will learn about the second step of the Client Catalyst System. In the sections that follow, you will learn about Catalysts, the critical role they play in helping you reach highly qualified clients, and how to search for and select the right Catalysts.

Note that the numbering associated with each "sub-step" listed in this chapter begins with "2" (e.g., 2.1, 2.1.1) to remind you of its position in the five steps of the Client Catalyst System. The numbered "sub-steps" identify the actions that you must take to implement Step 2 of the Client Catalyst System.

What Is A Catalyst?

By now you have encountered several references to the word Catalyst in this book. You have undoubtedly noticed that the system that you are learning about in this part of the book, the Client Catalyst System, also contains that word.

In chemistry, a catalyst is a substance that increases the rate of a chemical reaction without itself undergoing any permanent chemical change. But what is a Catalyst in the context of this book?

In this book, the term Catalyst refers to an individual who facilitates access to your prospective clients, without personally participating in the introduction process.

More specifically, a Catalyst is an individual who possesses the right qualifications, characteristics, and knowledge to help you to identify and connect with highly qualified prospective clients in ways that elevate you above your competition.

Why Use a Catalyst?

In their haste to sell consulting work, many new and less experienced consultants take it upon themselves to contact potential clients directly, often with little forethought or advance notice. This approach fails in most cases, simply because business is not geometry; the shortest path to highly qualified prospective clients is never a straight line!

Any seasoned consultant can attest to the fact that approaching decision-makers "cold," without investing the time and effort that is necessary to learn about them and to differentiate yourself from your competitors, is a guaranteed shortcut to failure.

Many professionals rely on referrals to overcome these challenges. Admittedly, referrals are one of the best ways to generate leads and connect with perspective clients. However, the majority of professionals use referrals incorrectly.

The fact is that a referral is nothing more than the opportunity to knock on your prospective client's proverbial door. Once the door is open, you must deliver something of value to your prospective client to keep the door open. Unfortunately, this is where the majority of professionals fail. They simply "ride the coattails" of the referring party to establish a connection with their prospective clients, and then proceed directly to "pitching" their products and services. In other cases, many professionals expect the referring party to take the initiative to present their merits, to share positive insights about their character and competence, or to endorse or recommend them to prospective clients. The simple fact is that most referring parties will avoid such actions because they prefer not to jeopardize their reputations or relationships.

The Client Catalyst System helps you to avoid these and other pitfalls associated with using referrals. In fact, this system's exceptional effectiveness is in part due to the fact that a Catalyst is much more than just a source of referrals. An ideal Catalyst provides you with *Six Catalyst Advantages* that help you to connect with highly qualified prospective clients in ways that elevate you above the competition. These advantages are:

1. Connections
2. Levers
3. Intelligence
4. Evaluations
5. Name Recognition
6. Timing Input

Use the acronym CLIENT to help you remember these advantages. The following sections briefly describe these advantages and their significance.

Connections

An ideal Catalyst provides you with the means to connect with highly qualified prospective clients. This is one of the cardinal functions of a Catalyst.

Levers

An ideal Catalyst provides you with insights about the core values and beliefs, ambitions, and passions of your prospective clients. These insights help you to better understand their intentions, motivations, and apprehensions, and also serve as "Value Levers" that you can use to influence your prospective clients. Access to such insights is an invaluable asset that the majority of your competitors lack.

Intelligence

An ideal Catalyst provides you with "Personal Intelligence," which refers to non-public information about your prospective clients that is usually limited to individuals who are personally familiar with them.

Personal Intelligence includes information about a person's preferences, habits, and routines, as well as what is most important to that person at present (e.g., upcoming product or service launches, projects in distress, important family matters, personal goals, and aspirations).

A firm grasp of Personal Intelligence empowers you to understand and relate to your prospective clients at a more personal level.

Evaluations

In Step Four of the Client Catalyst System, you will learn how to connect with highly qualified prospective clients in a way that elevates you above your competition. An ideal Catalyst provides you with feedback and evaluations of your approach in this critical step to help you succeed.

Name Recognition

An ideal Catalyst is a highly regarded member of your prospective client's community. When you connect with your prospective clients in Step Four of the Client Catalyst System, they become more receptive to connecting with you because of your association with the highly regarded Catalyst. In essence, the name of an ideal Catalyst is often the perfect "door opener."

Timing Input

An ideal Catalyst helps you to plan the timing of your initial contact with your prospective clients to coincide with when they may benefit most from your services. This is often a critical success factor in selling consulting services.

Clearly, using an ideal Catalyst to facilitate your access to highly qualified clients has the potential to elevate you above your competition. However, not all Catalysts are "ideal." In fact, you must evaluate each potential Catalyst deliberately and systematically to identify those that are most qualified to assist you. We discuss how to evaluate potential Catalysts later in this chapter.

In the following sections, we discuss how to search for, identify, and qualify potential Catalysts to help you reach highly qualified prospective clients.

2.1 Search for Catalysts

The most important factor that enables a Catalyst to facilitate your access to highly qualified prospective clients is his or her *knowledge* about them.

An effective Catalyst would possess Personal Intelligence and direct knowledge about the personal, professional, and organizational concerns of your prospective clients. An effective Catalyst would also be knowledgeable about the relevant issues affecting your prospective client's business, market, and industry.

Therefore, the most natural place to begin your search for a pool of Catalysts is the organizations where that knowledge and intelligence is concentrated.

2.1.1 Begin with the Seven Sources of INGRESS

There are countless organizations that serve as sources of knowledge and intelligence about a given community of prospective clients and their industry. Of these sources, seven have proven to be particularly fruitful in locating high quality Catalysts.

The Seven Sources of INGRESS™ that you should include in your search for a potential pool of Catalysts includes:

1. **Influence Centers:** This source includes organizations that influence your prospective client's industry as a whole. Examples include regulatory bodies that set industry standards, specify common and accepted best practices, and define procedural standards.
2. **News and Information Sources:** This source includes news media companies and publishers of news, blogs, and podcasts that cater to your prospective clients.
3. **Groups and Associations:** This source includes professional and industry associations, as well as user groups and communities where your prospective clients congregate.
4. **Referral and Networking Resources:** This source includes networking groups, referral communities, and venues that your prospective clients attend to conduct traditional "networking."

5. **Events, Meetings, and Conferences:** This source includes any organization that develops, markets, or produces industry events related to your prospective client's business.
6. **Service Providers:** This source includes any number of companies or individuals who provide a service to your prospective clients (this may include some of your peers and competitors, as well).
7. **Social Networks and Forums:** This source includes those social platforms that are most relevant to your prospective client's business, market, and industry (e.g., LinkedIn).

The acronym "INGRESS" can be helpful in remembering these sources of information and intelligence about your prospective clients.

Use a modern search engine such as Google to conduct an online search for *organizations* in each of the Seven Sources of INGRESS listed above. Since these organizations serve as an entry point for anyone interested in gaining knowledge and intelligence about your prospective client's business, industry, and market, you are likely to find high quality Catalysts working with or for these organizations.

What are some of the organizations in the Seven Sources of INGRESS listed above that cater to your prospective clients?

Free Online Resources

To save time when researching your potential pool of Catalysts among the Seven Sources of INGRESS, download a complementary *INGRESS Checklist* by visiting *NeverChaseClientsAgain.com/IngressChecklist*.

2.1.2 Identify Potential Catalysts

Once you have used the Seven Sources of INGRESS to identify a list of organizations, the next step is to identify potential Catalysts working with or for these organizations.

Continuing your online search, but this time focusing on each organization you identified in the previous step, search for individuals whose main function, business, or purpose is to:

- **Connect** your prospective clients with their customers.
- **Assist**, empower, or facilitate the success of your prospective clients.
- **Track**, study, or write about your prospective clients.
- **Assemble**, organize, or connect your prospective clients.
- **Lead** your prospective clients.
- **Yield** to or follow your prospective clients.
- **Serve** your prospective clients in some capacity.
- **Train**, educate, or inform your prospective clients

These individuals represent your pool of potential Catalysts (hence the use of the acronym "CATALYST" to help you remember their function).

Note that your business partners, suppliers, and vendors can also be potential Catalysts if they function in one of the capacities that we identified above.

Who are some of the individuals in your pool of potential Catalysts?

2.2 Select the Most Qualified Catalysts

Once you have identified a pool of potential Catalysts, the next step is to evaluate each Catalyst to identify the most qualified individuals. As we discussed earlier, not all Catalysts are well-positioned to assist you and unless you complete this step, you are likely to waste considerable time and effort pursuing or working with the wrong Catalysts.

The following section discusses the *qualifications t*hat you should consider in your evaluation of the individuals in your pool of potential Catalysts.

2.2.1 Understand Catalyst Qualifications

There are seven qualifications that you should use to evaluate each potential Catalyst. These *Seven Catalyst Qualifications*™ are:

1. Knowledgeable
2. Connected
3. Respected
4. Available
5. Inclined
6. Dependable
7. Relatable

The more of these qualifications your Catalysts possess, and the stronger their proficiency in each qualification, the more effectively and powerful they will be as your Catalysts. The following sections discuss each qualification in more detail.

Knowledgeable

This is by far the most important qualification for a potential Catalyst. A direct understanding of your prospective clients and their field is essential to facilitating your access to them.

A "knowledgeable" Catalyst must:

- Possess Personal Intelligence and direct knowledge about the personal, professional, and organizational concerns of your prospective clients.
- Understand the relevant issues affecting your prospective client's business, market, and industry.
- Have in-depth knowledge of the relevant facts, context, and connections that you need, especially when you cannot gain access to them on your own without investing a great deal of time, energy, and resources.

This qualification is the foundation that enables a Catalyst to provide you with the Six Catalyst Advantages we discussed earlier in the previous section. I cannot overstate the importance of this qualification. It must be your highest priority consideration when evaluating any potential Catalyst.

Connected

The breadth and depth of a Catalyst's network, as well as the strength of his or her relationships with each connection directly impacts the Catalyst's ability to connect you with highly qualified prospective clients.

A "well connected" Catalyst must either occupy a position of influence in your prospective client's community, or have strong connections and relationships with such influencers.

Respected

As discussed earlier, one of the Six Catalyst Advantages is name recognition. The more respected a potential Catalyst is in your prospective client's community, the more powerful the name recognition will be.

"Respected" Catalysts often play pivotal roles in your prospective client's community. You will learn more about this topic in the following sections that discuss searching for potential Catalysts.

Available

This is an essential qualification that requires your careful consideration. A Catalyst will not be effective in helping you reach prospective clients if he or she cannot invest the time to help you, or does not consider responsiveness to your requests a high priority.

There is an opportunity cost associated with waiting for a Catalyst that otherwise appears highly qualified, but who is not available to help you. In most cases, it is not worthwhile to wait for a Catalyst who is non-responsive, especially when you may be in a position to work with other available Catalysts.

A Catalyst who is "available" takes your calls, responds to your voicemail and e-mail messages within 48 hours, and provides you with other options if his or her schedule does not permit an immediate meeting.

Inclined

Whereas the qualification "available" (discussed above) concerns a Catalyst's responsiveness, this qualification concerns a Catalyst's willingness to help you.

Most seasoned professionals who have achieved a degree of success in business have done so because of the help of a mentor, advisor, or coach. If so, they may welcome an opportunity to "pay it forward" by helping you, especially if you offer them a powerful reason to do so.

A Catalyst who is highly "inclined" understands the value of investing time and effort to help others and exhibits a willingness to help.

Dependable

This qualification refers to a Catalyst's tendency to follow through with commitments and agreements. Unfortunately, this qualification is often difficult to gauge unless you have had prior interactions with a potential Catalyst. Nevertheless, you can formulate a preliminary opinion by closely observing a Catalyst's tendency to honor small agreements during your initial contact, such as replying to your e-mail or voicemail messages within a given time frame.

Similar to the qualification of "available" discussed above, there is an opportunity cost associated with relying on a Catalyst who is not dependable. Once again, you should reconsider working with such a Catalyst, especially when you have access to other potential Catalysts.

Relatable

To ensure your success in working with a Catalyst, you must choose only those individuals who feel compatible with your personality, working style, and moral and ethical viewpoints. Any "friction" between you and your potential Catalyst will negatively impact every other aspect of your mutual relationship.

Recall our discussion in Chapter Two regarding Empathy and the DISC Behavioral Styles. Your knowledge and understanding of your own Behavioral Style and that of a potential Catalyst can be a powerful advantage in determining how truly "relatable" a Catalyst is.

If you are interested in learning and applying the essential principles of the DISC Behavioral Style, obtain a copy of the special report I have created by visiting *NeverChaseClientsAgain.com/DISC*.

2.2.2 Evaluate Potential Catalysts

Your goal in this step is to identify those individuals in your pool of potential Catalysts who are most likely to possess the right knowledge and intelligence about your prospective clients, and who would be willing to share that knowledge and intelligence with you if you approach them properly.

Since *knowledge* is by far the most important qualification for a potential Catalyst, begin your evaluation with an Internet search to assess the level of knowledge and expertise of a potential Catalyst. For example, search for instances where a potential Catalyst:

- Has been interviewed, quoted, or mentioned in a publication that an organization in your Seven Sources of INGRESS has released.
- Has been published in newspapers, periodicals, or industry journals that cater to your prospective clients.
- Has posted blogs, articles, or "op-ed" content related to the personal, professional, and organizational concerns of your prospective clients.
- Has authored books, research papers, or special reports about the relevant issues affecting your prospective client's business, market, and industry.
- Has delivered keynote speeches, lectures, or training programs to members of your prospective client's community.
- Has attended industry events with other influencers in your prospective client's community.

Rate each individual in your pool of potential Catalysts based on the results of this research.

Note that the above research may also yield some relevant information that you can use to evaluate a potential Catalyst with respect to the "Connected" and "Respected" Catalyst Qualifications. However, I caution you against using unreliable measures such as a Catalyst's number of social media followers, Klout® score, or number of LinkedIn contacts in your evaluation of that Catalyst.

To properly evaluate a Catalyst with respect to the remaining Catalyst Qualifications (Connected, Respected, Available, Inclined, Dependable, and Relatable), you must personally interact with that Catalyst and with members of your own personal network.

However, evaluating a potential Catalyst based on the results of your research into their knowledge and expertise about your prospective clients is often sufficient to create a "shortlist" of the top three, most qualified Catalysts. This shortlist identifies the Catalysts who you will attempt to engage in Step Three of the Client Catalyst System that is described in the next chapter.

Of the individuals in your pool of potential Catalysts, who are best qualified to be on your shortlist? Based on your research, who are the top three most qualified candidates that you will engage in the next step of the Client Catalyst System?

Summary

- A Catalyst is an individual who facilitates access to your prospective clients, without personally participating in the introduction process.
- Business is not geometry; the shortest path to your highly qualified prospective clients is never a straight line.
- The majority of professionals use referrals incorrectly.

- An ideal Catalyst provides you with Six Catalyst Advantages that help you to connect with highly qualified prospective clients in ways that elevate you above the competition. These advantages are: (1) Connection, (2) Levers, (3) Intelligence, (4) Evaluations, (5) Name Recognition, and (6) Timing Input.
- The most important factor that enables a Catalyst to facilitate your access to highly qualified prospective clients is his or her knowledge about your prospective clients.
- The Seven Sources of INGRESS are the most natural places to begin your search for a pool of Catalysts. They include: (1) Influence Centers, (2) News and Information Sources, (3) Groups and Associations, (4) Referral and Networking Resources, (5) Events, Meetings, and Conferences, (6) Service Providers, and (7) Social Networks and Forums.
- To save time when researching your potential pool of Catalysts among the Seven Sources of INGRESS, download a complementary *INGRESS Checklist* by visiting *NeverChaseClientsAgain.com/IngressChecklist*.
- To identify a pool of potential Catalysts, search for individuals whose main function, business, or purpose is to Connect, Assist, Track, Assemble, Lead, Yield, Serve, or Train (CATLYST) your prospective clients.
- Evaluate each potential Catalyst using the Seven Catalyst Qualifications: (1) Knowledgeable, (2) Connected, (3) Respected, (4) Available, (5) Inclined, (6) Dependable, and (7) Relatable.
- Choose only an individual as a Catalyst who is compatible with your personality, working style, and moral and ethical viewpoints. Any "friction" between you and your potential Catalyst will negatively impact every other aspect of your mutual relationship.

- Identify those individuals in your pool of potential Catalysts who are most likely to possess the right knowledge and intelligence about your prospective clients, and who would be willing to share that knowledge and intelligence with you if you approach them properly.
- Knowledge is by far the most important qualification for a potential Catalyst.

CHAPTER SIX

STEP 3. ENGAGE CATALYSTS

In the last chapter, you identified a pool of potential Catalysts and evaluated the individuals in that pool to develop a "shortlist" of the top three, most qualified Catalysts. The next step in the Client Catalyst System is to engage those Catalysts in order to motivate at least one of them to facilitate your access to highly qualified prospective clients.

In the sections that follow, you will learn how to facilitate access to your most qualified Catalysts, how to determine what to offer them to add value to their lives, and how to present that offering of value in a way that motivates them to assist you.

Note that the numbering associated with each "sub-step" listed in this chapter begins with "3" (e.g., 3.1, 3.1.1) to remind you of its position in the five steps of the Client Catalyst System. The numbered "sub-steps" identify the actions that you must take to implement Step 3 of the Client Catalyst System.

3.1 Facilitate Access to Your Catalysts

As we discussed in the previous chapter, the shortest path to highly qualified prospective clients is never a straight line. The same is true of the shortest path to your most qualified Catalysts. Stated differently, you must not take it upon yourself to approach your potential Catalysts directly without first investing sufficient time and effort to learn about them, or without first obtaining a referral from someone they respect.

You must remember that your most qualified Catalysts are often busy, prominent, and in-demand professionals. Unless you find a way to differentiate yourself from others vying for their attention, they will be unlikely to honor your requests for contact.

In essence, your goal is to locate an "interim" Catalyst to facilitate your access to your most qualified Catalysts. Although this may appear to be a "circular argument" at first, it is not. You do not need to repeat the work you have completed so far to locate an interim Catalyst.

Choose a Catalyst from your list of top three, most qualified Catalysts, and follow this simple three-step process:

1. Find a contact in your network who knows the most qualified Catalyst that you have chosen to contact first.
2. Ask that contact for advice about the Catalyst.
3. Ask for permission to mention that contact's name when approaching the Catalyst.

The following sections briefly discuss each of these steps.

3.1.1 Find a Contact Who Knows Your Catalyst

The easiest way to identify a contact who knows your chosen Catalyst is to search your online professional network (e.g., LinkedIn). Your goal in this step is to locate a contact who can provide Personal Intelligence about the Catalyst that you have chosen to contact. As discussed in Chapter Five, Personal Intelligence refers to non-public information about your Catalyst that is usually limited to individuals who are personally familiar with him or her.

3.1.2 Ask Your Contact for Advice

Ask your contact for help in understanding the most qualified Catalyst that you have chosen to contact. Your goal in this step is gather as much Personal Intelligence about the Catalyst as possible. Bear in mind that unless you ask your contacts directly and specifically, they are unlikely to volunteer the type of information you need to gather.

Asking for Personal Intelligence conveys several important messages to your contacts:

1. It shows your sincere interest in learning more about your chosen Catalyst.
2. It communicates your intentions to be thoughtful and well-prepared, and to make meaningful contact with your chosen Catalyst.
3. It indicates to your contacts that you intend to "make them look good" when you approach your chosen Catalyst.

The last point above is a common subconscious concern for the majority of referrers. By alleviating this concern, you empower your contacts to agree to your final request to facilitate access to your most qualified Catalysts.

3.1.2 Ask for Permission to Mention Names

You must clearly explain to your contact that you are not asking for an endorsement or a recommendation; only permission to mention that contact's name when approaching the Catalyst who you have chosen to contact. You must also clearly explain that you will take all necessary actions to connect with your chosen Catalyst, and that you will not burden your contact further in any way.

By providing you with Personal Intelligence and their permission to mention their names when you approach your most qualified Catalyst, your contacts essentially act as "interim" Catalysts.

3.2 Develop an Offering of PURE Value

In order to differentiate yourself from everyone else vying for the attention of your most qualified Catalysts, you must develop an offering of PURE Value™ to present to them. You can accomplish this goal using the Personal Intelligence your "interim" Catalysts provided to you in the previous step.

What Is An Offering?

In the context of this book, an "Offering" can be anything that you possess, can attain, or can make happen that will be of value to someone else.

It is not necessary for an Offering to directly relate to the recipient's business or occupation. An Offering can be, and in many case should be, something that is of a personal nature.

Bear in mind that the effectiveness or *perceived* value of an Offering does not necessarily depend on the *actual* value or the success of your Offering to generate a specific outcome. What matters most is that you have:

- Invested time and effort to understand a recipient's needs, concerns, and desires.
- Taken the initiative to find a way to add value to your recipient's life.
- Made an effort to do something for your recipients before asking for anything in return.

Examples of potential Offerings include an expression of gratitude, empathetic listening and reflection, introductions to new business relationships, sales leads, and business books. Note that not all Offerings are physical in form, and that many are cost-free.

What Is PURE Value?

PURE is an acronym that identifies the conditions under which a recipient will perceive what you offer as highly valuable. An offer of PURE value is:

- **Personal:** It is not generic. It applies personally to the recipient. It is not intended for the recipient's organization. It can be related to the recipient's personal or professional life. It is not inappropriate or intimate in nature.
- **Unexpected:** It is something that the recipient does not expect to receive from you or others in your position.
- **Relevant:** It is relevant to the needs, concerns, and desires of the recipient, especially if they are pressing at the moment.
- **Exceptional:** It exceeds the expectations of the recipient.

Bear in mind that even when your offer meets the conditions above, the recipient is the sole judge of its perceived value. The last condition, "Exceptional," is a reminder of this fact that focuses your attention on developing offers that exceed the expectations of the recipients.

To develop an Offering of PURE value for your chosen Catalyst, use the Personal Intelligence your "interim" Catalysts provided to you in the previous step to consider the intersection between your Catalyst's possible needs and what you possess, can attain, or can make happen that will be of value to that Catalyst.

Example Offerings of PURE Value

The following are examples of what you might offer to your most qualified Catalysts that might be of value to them:

- Can you connect them with someone in your network who might be able to help them to accomplish a goal or achieve something that they value?
- Can you provide them with an opportunity to fulfill an emotional need or desire?

- Can you help a charitable causes, specific charities, or nonprofit organizations that they value or are involved with?
- Can you take an action that brings your background or professional experience to bear on an issue or a goal that they are concerned with?
- Can you help them find new customers or clients?
- Can you provide them with tips or strategies for improving or succeeding in their business?
- Can you provide them intelligence or knowledge that would help them to advance their interests?
- Can you provide them with gifts of knowledge such as books?
- Can you help them form a mutually beneficial alliance with companies or businesses that serve their market?
- Can you provide them with news or intelligence about their competitors?
- Can you provide them with leads that would help them to get more customers, more members, or more clients?

Note that many of the examples above are either items with monetary value that your Catalysts rarely receive free of charge, or they are items of no monetary value that your Catalysts rarely receive from business associates. Offerings such as the ones listed above often meet the "Unexpected" and "Exceptional" conditions that lead your Catalyst to perceive them as PURE Value Offerings.

What are some Offerings that you can obtain, create, or provide to your potential Catalysts that they may perceive as PURE Value Offerings? What are some Offerings that have no monetary value? What are some Offerings with perceived or actual monetary value that you could provide at minimal expense to yourself?

3.3 Present Your Offering of PURE Value to Catalysts

Once you have developed an Offering of PURE Value, you must contact your chosen Catalyst and present your Offering. How you choose to contact your Catalyst will depend on your personal preferences, the communication preferences of the Catalyst, and other factors that are difficult to predict or describe in this book.

However, you may choose to follow the simple three-step process below, which has proven effective in generating a positive response from potential Catalysts:

1. Construct and send an e-mail message to your chosen Catalyst to provide some context, to mention the name of the contacts that helped you to gain a better understanding of the Catalyst (refer to Step 1 above), and to set the Catalyst's expectations that you will follow up with a personal contact.
2. Contact your chosen Catalyst via telephone, remind him or her of the e-mail message and the context for your call, and suggest a brief meeting (or video call via Skype, FaceTime, or other means).
3. Meet with your chosen Catalyst in person, present your Offering of PURE Value, and discuss the possibility of working together.

Regardless of what process you follow to connect with your chosen Catalyst, it is most important that you retain control over the connection process. Under no circumstances should you ask or expect the contacts that referred you to this Catalyst to lead or participate in the connection process. However, if the referring contacts prefer to make a brief call or send a short e-mail message to set the stage, that would be entirely at their discretion.

Free Online Resources

There are many other approaches for contacting a potential Catalyst. I am continuously researching and updating an inventory of approaches that have proven effective in practice. To download a copy of the latest inventory of successful approaches, as well as sample e-mail messages that you can use to initiate contact with your chosen Catalyst or prospective clients, please visit *NeverChaseClientsAgain.com/FirstContact*.

3.4 Verify Catalyst's Qualifications and Intent

As you interact with your chosen Catalyst, continue to observe and collect information that can assist you in evaluating that Catalyst in the Seven Catalyst Qualifications we discussed in the previous chapter. If you recall, you evaluated individuals in your pool of potential Catalysts to identify your top three, most qualified Catalysts. Your evaluation was primarily based on your research into their knowledge about your prospective clients.

As we discussed in the previous chapter, in order to evaluate your Catalysts on all seven of the Catalyst Qualifications, you must interact with them. Based on your observations and interactions, confirm and update your qualifications ratings for your Catalysts in order to avoid wasting time and effort on those individuals who show signs of disinclination to help you, lack availability, or do not feel relatable.

No matter how attractive the knowledge and relationships that a chosen Catalyst might possess, he or she may not be a suitable choice if your ratings of his or her qualifications are unfavorable.

In addition, once you have presented your PURE Value Offering to your chosen Catalyst, you must verify that he or she will in fact assist you in reaching highly qualified prospective clients. This verification is essential because you cannot *assume* that your chosen Catalyst will actually help you.

Similar to your approach with the contacts who introduced you to your chosen Catalyst (refer to Step 1 above), you must clearly explain to your Catalyst that you are not asking for an endorsement or a recommendation; only permission to mention his or her name when approaching your prospective clients. You must also clearly explain that you will take all necessary actions to connect with your prospective clients, and that you will not burden your Catalyst further in any way.

Bear in mind that you may need to repeat Steps 1 through 4 for every one of your top three, most qualified Catalysts until you secure a suitable Catalyst who is willing, able, and qualified to help you to reach your prospective clients.

When you have successfully secured a suitable Catalyst, you are ready to move to the next step in the Client Catalyst System, and to identify and present a PURE Value Offering to your highly qualified clients. We discuss this step in the next chapter.

Summary

- You must not take it upon yourself to approach your potential Catalysts directly without first investing sufficient time and effort to learn about them, or without first obtaining a referral from someone they respect.
- Facilitate your access to a chosen Catalyst from your list of top three, most qualified Catalysts by: (1) finding a contact in your network who knows the Catalyst that you have chosen to contact first, (2) asking that contact for advice about the Catalyst, and (3) asking for permission to mention that contact's name when approaching the Catalyst.

- In order to differentiate yourself from everyone else vying for the attention of your most qualified Catalysts, you must develop an offering of PURE value to present to them.
- An "Offering" can be anything that you possess, can attain, or can make happen that will be of value to someone else. The effectiveness or *perceived* value of an Offering does not necessarily depend on the *actual* value or the success of your Offering to generate a specific outcome.
- PURE is an acronym that identifies the conditions under which a recipient will perceive what you offer as highly valuable. An offer of PURE value is: (1) Personal, (2) Unexpected, (3) Relevant, and (4) Exceptional.
- As you interact with your chosen Catalyst, continue to observe and collect information that can assist you in evaluating that Catalyst in the Seven Catalyst Qualifications we discussed in the previous chapter.
- To download a copy of the latest inventory of successful approaches, as well as sample e-mail messages that you can use to initiate contact with your chosen Catalyst or prospective clients, please visit *NeverChaseClientsAgain.com/FirstContact*.
- Once you have presented your PURE Value Offering to your chosen Catalyst, you must verify that he or she will in fact assist you in reaching highly qualified prospective clients.

CHAPTER SEVEN

STEP 4. ELEVATE YOURSELF

Once you have engaged and secured the help of a qualified Catalyst, the next step of the Client Catalyst System is to identify potential clients and to present them with an Offering that elevates you above your competition in their minds. This process is similar to the one described in the previous chapter, which you followed to connect with your Catalyst.

In the sections that follow, you will learn how to seek the assistance of your Catalyst to identify highly qualified clients, develop an Offering of PURE Value, and connect with your prospective clients to present your Offering.

Note that the numbering associated with each "sub-step" listed in this chapter begins with "4" (e.g., 4.1, 4.2, 4.2.1) to remind you of its position in the five steps of the Client Catalyst System. The numbered "sub-steps" identify the actions that you must take to implement Step 4 of the Client Catalyst System.

4.1 Identify Highly Qualified Clients

Because your Catalyst possesses extensive knowledge and intelligence about your prospective clients, he or she is uniquely positioned to help you identify those clients who meet the majority of your PATRONS Criteria. You defined the PATRONS Criteria that identify your highly qualified prospective clients as part of your activities in Step 1 of the Client Catalyst System.

Your goal in this step should be to identify as many highly qualified prospective clients as possible. To leverage your Catalyst's knowledge to accomplish this goal, follow the four-step process outlined below.

1. Arrange a meeting with your Catalyst to discuss your client pursuit strategy and activities.
2. In preparation for your meeting, draft a document that summarizes your PATRONS Criteria and provides a listing

of several specific organizations and professionals that meet the majority of those criteria. If you recall, you prepared such a list as part of your activities in Step 1 of the Client Catalyst System.
3. During your meeting with your Catalyst, review the document that you prepared in the previous step, discuss your PATRONS Criteria, and ask your Catalyst for help in identifying organizations and individuals who meet your criteria and whom you should pursue as highly qualified prospective clients.
4. For each highly qualified prospective client that your Catalyst helps you to identify, ask him or her for additional information to better understand that prospective client. Learn as much as possible about your prospective client's business, personal, and other interests, which will be crucial to your success in developing an Offering of PURE Value. Focus on the prospective client's Value Levers, communication preferences, and Personal Intelligence. Seek your Catalyst's input regarding the timing of your initial contact with your prospective clients to ensure that it coincides with when they may benefit the most from your services (or when they may be most inclined to buy your services).

Your Catalyst is unlikely to volunteer information of this type unless you ask for it specifically and directly. Therefore, it is vitally important that you lead and direct your meeting with your Catalyst and prompt him or her with specific, open-ended questions to elicit the information that you need.

In addition, you must clearly explain to your Catalyst that you are committed to learning more about each prospective client so that you can provide him or her with an Offering of PURE Value.

Your Catalyst will most likely recall his or her own experiences in connecting with you, and will appreciate your commitment to adding value to your prospective clients.

You must also explain to your Catalyst that you are not asking for an endorsement or a recommendation; only permission to mention your Catalyst's name when approaching each prospective client. Answer any question your Catalyst may have about the process that you will follow to connect with prospective clients, and work diligently to alleviate his or her concerns about the process.

Once your Catalyst has helped you to develop a list of highly qualified prospective clients and provided you with the additional intelligence you need, the next step is to develop an Offering that differentiates you from your competitors.

How will you arrange and conduct your meeting with your Catalyst? What questions will you pose to your Catalyst to elicit the information you need about your prospective clients? How will you explain your approach to your Catalyst so as to alleviate his or her concerns about making a referral?

Free Online Resources

Your success in orchestrating and conducting your initial meeting with a potential Catalyst is critical to leveraging his or her knowledge, position, and relationships to reach highly qualified prospective clients. To prepare for your initial meeting, download a complementary *Catalyst Meeting Checklist* by visiting *NeverChaseClientsAgain.com/CatalystMeeting*.

4.2 Develop an Offering of PURE Value

In order to differentiate yourself from everyone else vying for the attention of your highly qualified clients, you must develop an

Offering of PURE Value to present to them. You can accomplish this goal using the Value Lever information and the Personal Intelligence your Catalyst provided to you in the previous step.

The process is virtually identical to the one that you followed in Step 3 of the Client Catalyst System to develop an Offering of PURE Value for your Catalyst. As discussed earlier, your Offering can be anything that your prospective clients find of value. It is not necessary for your Offering to directly relate to your prospective clients' business or occupation. Your Offering can be, and in many case should be, something that is of a personal nature.

If necessary, consider conducting your own research to learn more about your prospective clients and their recent public and professional activities. Combine the results of your own research with the intelligence your Catalyst has supplied to improve your Offering of PURE Value.

4.2.1 Think REMARKABLE

Your options are limitless with respect to the specific Offering that you can develop for each of your prospective clients. There are, however, ten categories of Offerings that have proven to be effective in eliciting a high perception of value from prospective clients. The names of these ten categories form the acronym REMARKABLE, and they are as follows:

1. Relationships
2. Emotional Fulfillment
3. Major Interests
4. Actions
5. Revenue Ideas
6. Knowledge
7. Alliances

8. Beating the Competition
9. Leads
10. Expansion Ideas

As you consider your options for developing an Offering for each of your prospective clients, review the list of REMARKABLE categories above and brainstorm ideas for each category. Use the following mnemonic to help you remember the objectives in this step: *"Offerings of PURE Value are often REMARKABLE."*

The sections that follow discuss each category in more detail.

Relationships

Imagine your prospective client's business as a value chain consisting of customers, service providers, suppliers, and distributors. Each link in this value chain represents an opportunity for improvement. How can you help your prospective client realize those improvements though connections and introductions to others in your network?

In addition, consider your prospective client's personal needs, goals, and concerns. How can you use your personal and professional network to help them to accomplish a goal, alleviate a concern, or obtain something that they need?

Emotional Fulfillment

Each of your prospective clients has individual emotional needs and desires, each of which is an opportunity to help your prospective clients feel more fulfilled. How can you help your prospective clients to experience the emotions they seek, meet an emotional need, or fulfill an emotional desire?

Major Interests

The majority of your prospective clients have major interests and passions other than business. Some are involved with charitable causes, community programs, or nonprofit organizations. How can you help to support your prospective client's major interests?

Actions

The old adage "actions speak louder than words" is the cornerstone of this category. What actions can you take that bring your background and professional experience to bear on an issue or goal that your prospective clients are concerned with?

Revenue Ideas

Your prospective clients generate revenue for their business by serving customers or clients. How can you help them serve more customers or clients faster or more efficiently? How can you help them to find new sources of revenue that they may have not considered before? What tips or strategies can you share with them to help them to improve or succeed in their business?

Knowledge

Besides your specialized knowledge in your subject matter, what you know can be of great value to your prospective clients. Consider your personal interests and hobbies, past experiences, travels, passions, and pastimes. What other knowledge do you possess that your prospective clients might find valuable or interesting?

The knowledge you offer does not necessarily need to originate with you. What intelligence or knowledge have others produced or accumulated that would help your prospective clients to advance their interests? What gifts of knowledge, such as books, can you give to your prospective clients?

Alliances

Examine the market your prospective client's business competes in. What other businesses serve the same customer base with products that do not compete with those of your prospective client? These companies may represent opportunities for alliances and partnerships. How can you help your prospective clients to form a mutually beneficial alliance with companies or businesses that serve their market?

Beating the Competition

Your prospective clients are always searching for opportunities to gain an advantage over their competition. Analyze your prospective clients' business models and identify their potential competitors. How can you provide them with news or intelligence about their competitors that would provide your prospective clients with an advantage over their competitors, or eliminate a competitor's advantage?

Leads

Examine the market that your prospective clients serve. Who are their ideal customers, members, or subscribers? How can you provide your prospective clients with leads that would help them to get more customers, members, or clients?

Expansion Ideas

Analyze your prospective client's products and services to identify new applications or uses for those products and services.

Consider new markets or territories that represent expansion opportunities for those products and services. Think of ideas for combining your prospective client's products or services with those of another company to create a new, more competitive product or service. How can you help your prospective clients think through these opportunities?

It is important to remember that the *perceived* value of your Offering does not necessarily depend on its *actual* value or its success in generating a specific outcome. What matters most is that you have:

- Invested time and effort to understand the needs, concerns, and desires of your prospective clients.
- Taken the initiative to find a way to add value to your prospective clients.
- Made an effort to do something for your prospective clients before asking for anything in return.

What is an Offering that will help you to rise above the crowd and motivate your prospective clients to give you their time and attention? Does your Offering meet the conditions of PURE Value? Is your Offering a REMARKABLE offer?

4.2.2 Consult Your Catalyst

Once you have identified an Offering of PURE Value for your prospective clients, you should consult your Catalyst to confirm that, based on his or her knowledge of your prospective clients, they will perceive your Offering as highly valuable. This confirmation step will not require much effort, but it can help you to avoid investing time and effort on an ineffective Offering. You only get one chance to make a first impression with your prospective clients, so it is in your best interest to develop the best Offering that you can from the onset.

In addition, your Catalyst will regard you in a positive light because of your commitment to being prepared, adding value to your prospective clients, and approaching the referral your Catalyst has made in a very professional manner. Over time, this will lead your Catalyst to trust you more completely.

As you share your planned Offering with your Catalyst, seek his or her feedback. Confirm your understanding of the prospective clients' Personal Intelligence and Value Levers, which were at the foundation for your choosing that particular Offering. If your Catalyst provides you with feedback on your Offering, be sure to consider and incorporate that feedback into your Offering to make it more effective.

If you conducted your own research to learn more about your prospective clients and their recent public and professional activities in the previous step, use this opportunity to share your findings with your Catalyst to help him or her become better informed.

Finally, use this opportunity to keep your Catalyst informed about your approach and progress, and to alleviate any concerns he or she might have about the process.

How will you confirm your Offering of PURE Value with your Catalyst? How will you seek your Catalyst's feedback? What additional information could you share with your Catalyst to add value to his or her life?

4.3 Present Your Offering to Your Prospective Client

Once you have developed an Offering of PURE Value and consulted your Catalyst, you must contact your prospective client and present your Offering. How you choose to carry out this step will depend on your personal preferences, the communication preferences of your prospective client, and other factors that are difficult to predict or describe in this book.

However, you may choose to follow the simple three-step process below, which has proven effective in generating a positive response from prospective clients:

1. Construct and send an e-mail message to your prospective client to provide some context, to mention the name of your Catalyst, and to set the expectation that you will follow up with a personal contact.
2. Contact your prospective client via telephone, remind him or her of the e-mail message and the context for your call, and suggest a brief meeting (or video call via Skype, FaceTime, or other means).
3. Meet with your prospective client in person, whenever possible, present your Offering of PURE Value, and explore the possibility of working together. For more details on this step, refer to the next chapter.

Regardless of what process you follow to connect with your prospective client, take note of the following important considerations:

- It is vitally important that you retain control over the connection process. Under no circumstances should you ask or expect your Catalyst to lead or participate in the connection process. However, if your Catalyst prefers to make a brief call or send a short e-mail message to set the stage, that would be entirely at his or her discretion.
- Before each contact with your prospective client, take the necessary time to prepare. Review your prospective client's Value Levers and Personal Intelligence information.

Revisit records of any past interactions. Check your hygiene and appearance prior to in-person meetings.
- Whenever possible, honor the communications preference of your prospective clients. Always proofread your written communications. Note any commitments and agreements, and share them with your prospective clients when appropriate.

How will you conduct your initial contact with your prospective clients? How will you retain control over the process of connecting with and presenting your Offering of PURE Value to your prospective clients?

Free Online Resources

There are many other approaches for your initial contact with prospective clients. I am continuously researching and updating an inventory of approaches that have proven effective in practice. To download a copy of the latest inventory of successful approaches, as well as sample e-mail messages that you can use to initiate contact with your prospective clients, please visit *NeverChaseClientsAgain.com/FirstContact*.

4.4 Verify Client's Perception of Value

When you connect with your prospective client and present your Offering of PURE Value, you must verify that he or she has indeed *perceived* your Offering to be valuable. You cannot simply *assume* that your Offering is as impactful as you hoped. Verifying the perceived value of your Offering is an important step because your prospective client's circumstances, needs, and goals may have changed without your Catalyst's awareness. The Personal

Intelligence and Value Levers that served as the foundation of your Offering may have been inaccurate.

In addition, your goal in developing and presenting an Offering to your prospective clients is to actually deliver something of value to them, not to complete an item on your "to-do" list. Therefore, if your Offering proves to be ineffective or is of little perceived value to your prospective clients, you must correct its shortcomings and develop a better Offering.

Your persistence in this regard will pay dividends many times over. Your efforts demonstrate your good character and your commitment to delivering value to your prospective clients before asking for anything. They will appreciate your tenacity because your approach is worlds apart from that of your competitors; it is well-informed, professional, and the polar opposite of "salesy."

Once your Offering has succeeded in delivering value to your prospective client, you are well-positioned to take the next step in the Client Catalysts System, which is to explore opportunities to work with your prospective client.

Summary

- Your Catalyst possesses extensive knowledge and intelligence about your prospective clients. Seek his or her advice to identify as many highly qualified prospective clients (who meet the majority of your PATRONS Criteria) as possible.
- To prepare for your initial meeting with a potential Catalyst, download a complementary *Catalyst Meeting Checklist* by visiting *NeverChaseClientsAgain.com/CatalystMeeting*.
- Ask your Catalyst for additional information to better understand your prospective clients. Learn as much as

possible about your prospective client's business, personal, and other interests, as well as his or her Value Levers, communication preferences, and Personal Intelligence.

- Explain to your Catalyst the approach and the process that you will follow to deliver an Offering of PURE Value to your prospective clients.
- Explain to your Catalyst that you are not asking for an endorsement or a recommendation; only permission to mention your Catalyst's name when approaching each prospective client.
- Use the Value Lever information and the Personal Intelligence that your Catalyst provided to you to develop an Offering of PURE Value for your prospective clients. When brainstorming the categories of Offerings, think REMARKABLE: Relationships, Emotional fulfillment, Major Interests, Actions, Revenue Ideas, Knowledge, Alliances, Beating the Competition, Leads, and Expansion Ideas.
- Always consult your Catalyst to confirm that, based on his or her knowledge of your prospective clients, they will perceive your Offering as highly valuable.
- When connecting with your prospective client to present your Offering, it is vitally important that you retain control over the connection process. Under no circumstances should you ask or expect your Catalyst to lead or participate in the connection process.
- When you present your Offering of PURE Value to your prospective clients, verify that he or she has indeed *perceived* your Offering to be valuable.
- To download a copy of the latest inventory of successful approaches for your initial contact with prospective clients, as well as sample e-mail messages that you can use to

initiate contact with them, please visit *NeverChaseClientsAgain.com/FirstContact*.

CHAPTER EIGHT

STEP 5. EXPLORE OPPORTUNITIES

Once you have elevated yourself above your competitors by delivering an Offering of PURE Value to your prospective clients, and then confirmed that they have indeed perceived your Offering as valuable, your next step is to explore the opportunities to work with your prospective clients.

Your goal in this fifth step of the Client Catalyst System is to determine whether there are opportunities for you to provide your prospective clients with your professional services, to use the good will that you have developed with them to connect with other prospects, or to engage them as potential Catalysts. In the following sections, you will learn how to explore these opportunities.

Note that the numbering associated with each "sub-step" listed in this chapter begins with "5" (e.g., 5.1, 5.2) to remind you of its position in the five steps of the Client Catalyst System. The numbered "sub-steps" identify the actions that you must take to implement Step 5 of the Client Catalyst System.

5.1 Explore Opportunities to Serve Prospective Client

There are five distinct steps in exploring the possibility of providing your prospective client with professional services. Expressed in their simplest form, these five steps can be expressed as:

1. Engage
2. Listen
3. Frame
4. Envision
5. Commit

The following sections discuss each step in more detail.

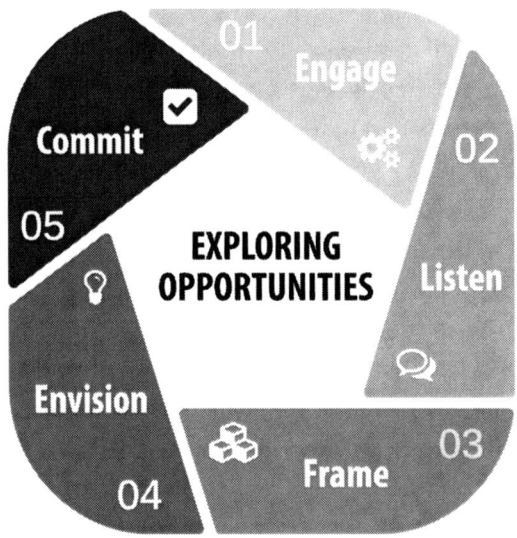

Engage

The first step in exploring the opportunities to serve your prospective clients is to engage them in a way that motivates them to not only begin a conversation with you, but also to feel comfortable with sharing and acknowledging the issues that are important to them.

By implementing the first four steps in the Client Catalyst System, you will successfully connect with and engage your prospective client.

Listen

Once you successfully connect with and engage your prospective clients, you earn the right to *listen* and to engage them in a direct, mutual exploration of ideas.

Until this point in the Client Catalyst System, your knowledge and understanding of your prospective client's circumstances, needs, and goals have been based on indirect information that you have collected from your Catalyst or through your own research. You now have the opportunity to ask questions to gain knowledge and understanding about your prospective clients directly from the source.

In this step, you must listen actively, consciously, and intently to your prospective clients. Ask powerful questions, and confirm and validate what you hear in response. You must listen to what they say, and seek to understand what they leave unspoken. Your empathy will be a critical factor in this step.

Frame

Having listened to your prospective clients, and having understood and acknowledged the issues and problems they grapple with, you must help them to clarify and correlate the issues surrounding those problems, and to identify the root cause or the core issue that must be resolved.

Framing the core issue is in essence defining the main problem in solvable terms, while recognizing what matters most to your prospective clients.

Envision

Having defined the core issue, you must focus your efforts on envisioning a solution that helps your prospective clients to achieve the outcomes, goals, or circumstances that they value most. In this step of the process, you are not focused on *solving* the core issue; instead, you are focused on helping your prospective clients to understand their most-valued goals and outcomes, so that they can consciously commit to achieving them.

Bear in mind that it is possible for your prospective clients to choose *not* to solve a core issue, despite acknowledging its existence. They may decide that the effort that is necessary to resolve an issue outweighs the benefits.

Commit

In this step of the process, your goal is to ensure that your prospective clients understand the effort that is necessary to solve the core issue you identified in the previous step, and to find the determination to commit to resolving that issue.

You must be prepared to express the complexities, challenges, and risks involved with the effort with authenticity, integrity, and enthusiasm.

At the conclusion of this step, you and your prospective clients are ready to begin discussions about an engagement or a project to help them to implement the solution you envisioned.

5.2 Explore Opportunities to Connect with Others

As you explore the opportunities to serve your prospective clients with your professional services, you should simultaneously evaluate the possibilities of connecting them to others in your professional network.

By completing the first four steps of the Client Catalyst System, you have developed a degree of "good will" with your prospective clients. In essence, you have earned the right to *explore* a mutually beneficial professional relationship. Although they are by no means obligated or committed to building a professional relationship with you or your firm, your continued efforts to add value to your prospective clients will in practice increase the likelihood of developing such a professional relationship.

Connecting your prospective clients with others in your professional network is an effective way to accomplish that goal.

One beneficial side effect of this approach is that when you share your professional network with your prospective clients, they may feel more comfortable sharing their professional network with you.

As with any other industry and profession, your highly qualified prospective clients are undoubtedly connected with other professionals, many of whom are likely to be prospective clients who you may want to pursue. In that case, your highly qualified prospective client may be able to serve as an "interim" Catalyst to facilitate your access to other prospective clients in their professional network. Refer to Step 2 of the Client Catalyst System for more information about "interim" Catalysts.

In addition, if your highly qualified prospective clients meet the majority of the Seven Catalyst Qualifications, you may wish to approach them as you would a potential Catalyst (starting with Step 3 of the Client Catalyst System). Refer to Step 2 of the Client Catalyst System for a detailed discussion of the Seven Catalyst Qualifications.

Bear in mind that your highly qualified prospective clients may be better suited as "organizational" Catalysts who facilitate your access to other prospects within their own organizations, as opposed to general Catalysts with broader market and industry knowledge.

Summary

- There are three primary opportunities to explore with your prospective clients: to provide professional services, to connect with other professionals and prospects, and to engage them as potential Catalysts.

- There are five distinct steps in exploring the possibility of providing your prospective client with professional services. They are: (1) Engage, (2) Listen, (3) Frame, (4) Envision, and (5) Commit.
- By completing the first four steps of the Client Catalyst System, you have earned the right to explore a mutually beneficial professional relationship with your prospective clients. To build this professional relationship, you must continue to add value to them.
- Your highly qualified prospective clients are undoubtedly connected with other professionals, many of whom are likely to be prospective clients you may want to pursue.
- If your highly qualified prospective clients meet the majority of the Seven Catalyst Qualifications, you may wish to approach them as you would a potential Catalyst, starting with Step 3 of the Client Catalyst System.

PART THREE

STAY COMPETITIVE

In this part, you will discover how to master the skills that you have learned in this book, and what you must do on an ongoing basis to improve your efficiency in implementing the strategies, principles, and ideas it contains.

CHAPTER NINE

WHY PRACTICE DOES NOT MAKE PERFECT

I have always had a fascination with becoming a master marksman. I remember building a slingshot as a six-year-old boy and practicing my "craft" on unsuspecting sparrows flying around the backyard of our house. By the time I was nine years old, I could hit a metal can with my trusty slingshot from 50 yards away on the first try. A few years ago, I once again took up the "craft," but this time with firearms. However, after three years of practice, I still had not experienced the same advancement in skills as I experienced with my trusty slingshot.

I realized that in order to take my skills to the next level, I needed to first learn what was *not* working. I needed to learn what I did not know *that I did not know*, and for that, I needed the help of someone who *did* know what *I* did not know. In short, I needed a coach to first show me my blind spots, and then to help me to overcome them.

Fortunately, I was able to find and convince a highly trained marksman to coach me. After observing me in target practice for a few minutes, he asked me "How often do you practice?" I answered "At least once a week." He then replied "Well, that is your problem!"

Assuming that I had understood his meaning, I replied "So what you're suggesting is that I practice more often?" He paused for a moment and then said, "No. Your problem is that you practice the *wrong* things too often. The way you position yourself to hit your targets is ineffective. But I'm not surprised. It's such a popular approach to teach today. You can hardly pick up a book that doesn't teach it. But it's not the *best* way to hit your target, not by a long shot." I was beginning to regret following the advice in the marksmanship books I had recently read.

He then said, "To master this skill, you need to practice the *most effective* way to position yourself, not the most *popular* way. Practice does not make perfect; *perfect* practice makes perfect."

Following his advice, I have made significant improvements in my marksmanship skills over the past few months. It is clear to me now that without his coaching, his insights, and the new strategies that he shared with me, I would have never achieved those improvements. In all likelihood, I would have continued to make meager improvements that would have rewarded me just enough to keep "practicing," but not enough to reach to my full potential.

What about you? What popular strategies are you "practicing" to find new clients and to grow your firm that prevent you from reaching your full potential?

Hit Your Targets

The Client Catalyst System that you have learned in this book is a proven system that is quite possibly the fastest, the easiest, and the most effective way to get new clients. It arms you with the right ammunition and positions you perfectly to hit your target clients. However, you cannot master this system by merely reading about it in this book. You must practice it in actuality.

Of course, you can expect to make mistakes as you put the Client Catalyst System into practice. Mistakes are a part of the learning process and can be of great benefit, if you can learn from your mistakes (or the mistakes of others, as we will discuss in a moment). Trial and error is certainly a valid strategy for improving your mastery of any system, as long as you are aware of and willing to invest the time and effort that is required by that strategy. Trial and error is the strategy that I used to develop and master the Client Catalyst System over a period of nearly 20 years.

Nevertheless, there is an important fact that you must bear in mind: *Success loves speed*. The faster that you can learn to implement and master the Client Catalyst System, the more successful you will be in getting highly qualified prospective clients to grow your firm.

That is precisely the reason why I have developed an online training course to provide you with the extra help and guidance that you need to avoid common mistakes and time-consuming trial and error. You can complete the course at your own pace over a weekend, and begin implementing the Client Catalyst System on Monday morning. In addition, you can revisit the training whenever you need to increase your efficiency and improve your effectiveness in implementing what you have learned. To learn more about this training course, visit *NeverChaseClientsAgain.com/Training*.

There are, of course, other ways to master the Client Catalyst System and to improve your efficiency in implementing the strategies, principles, and ideas outlined in this book. The sections that follow briefly discuss several options for you to consider.

Focus On Progress

Progress is better than perfection. Avoid getting bogged down in the attempted perfect execution of each step of the Client Catalyst System. Focus on completing the steps in the system from start to finish as quickly as possible. Make notes on your progress, and take time to reflect on your notes. Learn as much from what worked well as what did not. Build momentum by repeating the process again and again, and by making notes and reflecting on them each time.

Focus on progress, and you will gain mastery as a matter of course.

Cherish Your Catalyst

Treat your relationship with your Catalyst as your most important professional relationship. Guard it, nurture it, and embrace it. Make a point to continuously add value to your relationship. Treat your Catalyst as your most important client — someone under your protection.

Every minute that you invest with your Catalyst will save you hours when time matters most.

Get Two to Get Better

If having one Catalyst is good, having two is better. There is no reason why you must be content with only one Catalyst to help your reach highly qualified clients. If you can invest the time and effort to simultaneously nurture relationships with two Catalysts (refer to the previous point), then by all means find a second Catalyst.

Better still, introduce your Catalysts to each other. The synergies you can create for both your Catalysts and yourself can be incredibly powerful.

Improve Your Core

Improve your proficiency in the Three Core Qualifications discussed in Chapter Two, and you will improve your effectiveness in implementing the strategies, principles, and ideas you learned in this book.

Every step of the Client Catalyst System relies on your proficiency in one or more of the Three Core Qualifications. For instance:

- Demonstrating your commitment to your Catalyst and to your prospective clients by adding value (the second Core Qualification) is an integral element of the Client Catalyst System.
- Your Soft Skills (part of the third Core Qualification) are essential to your ability to influence your Catalyst and your prospective clients to work with you.
- Demonstrating the Five Critical Character Traits (the first Core Qualification) are prerequisites for engaging your Catalyst, elevating yourself above your competition, and exploring opportunities to serve your prospective clients (Steps 3, 4, and 5 of the Client Catalyst System, respectively).

Even a small improvement in your proficiency in each of the Three Core Qualifications will exponentially increase your success in finding highly qualified clients.

Learn From the Mistakes of Others

As discussed earlier, you can certainly learn from your own mistakes in implementing the Client Catalyst System. As with learning anything else through trial and error, the process can be slow, frustrating, and sometimes painful.

You can, of course, avoid some of the pain and frustration by learning from the mistakes of others. If you are interested in joining a private community of firm leaders, seasoned consultants, and your peers who are interested in learning from each other as they build and grow their consulting firms, visit *NeverChaseClientsAgain.com/LeadersForum*. It is one of the free benefits of being a reader of this book.

Team Up

Implement the Client Catalyst System as a firm leader and you can *grow* your consulting firm. Train and team up with other leaders in your firm to implement the system, and you can truly *transform* your consulting firm.

Train your entire business development team to implement the Client Catalyst System, and no one in your consulting firm will ever chase clients again.

Summary

- To master a skill, you need to practice the *most effective* way to accomplish its constituent steps, not the most *popular* way.

- Practice does not make perfect; *perfect* practice makes perfect.
- You cannot master the Client Catalyst System by merely reading about it in this book. You must practice it in actuality.
- *Success loves speed.* The faster that you can learn to implement and master the Client Catalyst System, the more successful you will be in getting highly qualified prospective clients to grow your firm.
- To access an online training course that can help you to avoid common mistakes and time-consuming trial and error in implementing the Client Catalyst System, visit *NeverChaseClientsAgain.com/Training*.
- Progress is better than perfection. Focus on progress, and you will gain mastery as a matter of course.
- Treat your relationship with your Catalyst as your most important professional relationship. Every minute that you invest with your Catalyst will save you hours when time matters most.
- If having one Catalyst is good, having two is better. If you can invest the time and effort to simultaneously nurture relationships with two Catalysts, then by all means find a second Catalyst.
- Improve your proficiency in the Three Core Qualifications discussed in Chapter Two, and you will improve your effectiveness in implementing the strategies, principles, and ideas you learned in this book.
- Avoid the pain and frustration of learning through trial and error by learning from the mistakes of others. Visit *NeverChaseClientsAgain.com/LeadersForum* to join a private community of firm leaders, seasoned consultants,

and your peers who are interested in learning from each other as they build and grow their consulting firms.
- Train and team up with other leaders in your firm to implement the Client Catalyst System, and you can truly *transform* your consulting firm.

Chapter Ten

Conclusion

As a consultant and a firm leader, you face many choices and challenges on your way to building a successful consulting firm. Perhaps the most critical of those choices and challenges is deciding when, where, and how to spend your scarcest resource -- your time. In order to succeed, you must find better ways to maximize your efficiency in conducting your firm's most critical functions, such as finding highly qualified clients to serve.

New marketing and lead generation strategies, such as content marketing and social media campaigns, promise great efficiencies in finding prospective clients for you. After all, you can easily outsource the majority of your firm's content marketing and social media activities. However, the overall return on your investment in these new strategies is often smaller than their promise.

The reason for this shortcoming is that many new marketing and lead generation strategies fail to consider an important fact about consulting. Consulting has always been, and will always remain, a business that is built on personal and professional relationships. Regardless of how you identify prospective clients, you cannot outsource the building of personal and professional relationships with them.

The ultimate efficiency in finding prospective clients is not gained by generating a larger number of contacts and leads with less effort; it is gained by increasing the speed with which you build personal and professional relationships with those prospective clients who are highly qualified.

The Client Catalyst System that you learned in the preceding chapters can help you to find a nearly unlimited supply of high-quality, prospective clients while simultaneously laying the foundation for building solid personal and professional relationships with them. For instance:

- When you use a Catalyst, you will discover your prospective client's Value Levers and Personal Intelligence. This information is not only critical to developing an Offering of PURE Value that motivates a prospective client to work with you, but it is also essential to building a stronger relationship with that person. It is highly unlikely that you will be able to obtain this information through publicly available resources or directly from your prospective client without a preexisting relationship.
- Using your Catalyst's name when connecting with your prospective client for the first time bestows a level of trust and credibility upon you and your connection request. In fact, most professionals respond positively to connection requests originating from colleagues of those whom they

trust, and they do so without the typical reluctance and apprehension that they may display when responding to someone that they do not recognize, know, or trust.
- By providing your prospective clients with an Offering of PURE Value before you ask for anything, you demonstrate your positive character and encourage reciprocity in them. In his seminal book *Influence: The Psychology of Persuasion*, Robert Cialdini identifies reciprocity as "one of the most potent of the weapons of influence around us." Increasing your influence with your prospective clients will predispose them to working with you.

Implementing the Client Catalyst System will provide you with the benefits listed above, as well as other benefits that can help you to begin your interactions with your prospective clients from a position of positive impact, implicit trust, and perceived credibility. As a result, you are more likely to succeed in building personal and professional relationships with your prospective clients, and you will do so much more efficiently than you would without using the Client Catalyst System.

Admittedly, implementing the steps in the system does require an investment of your time. As with learning any other system or process, you can expect to invest more time upfront, when you implement the steps in the system for the very first time.

However, the time investment required to execute the steps will decrease dramatically as you become more familiar with the system and complete the foundational steps of establishing your PATRONS Criteria, evaluating potential Catalysts, and engaging in a mutually beneficial relationship with a Catalyst (Steps 1 through 3 of the Client Catalyst System, respectively).

This initial investment of time will provide ongoing returns as you continue to work with your Catalyst to identify, reach, and connect with highly qualified prospective clients. The next step of the system (Step 4) that entails identifying a highly qualified prospective client, developing an Offering of PURE Value, and contacting that client to present your Offering can often be completed in as little as one day.

In addition, since your Catalyst will help you to identify a highly qualified prospective client who satisfies the majority of your PATRONS Criteria, it is very likely that you will be successful in proceeding quickly to Step 5 of the Client Catalyst System -- exploring opportunities to serve that prospective client.

In the last chapter, I provided you with additional tips and suggestions to help you to master the Client Catalyst System and to improve your efficiency in implementing its constituent steps. In addition, there are further resources at your disposal to help you to learn the Client Catalyst System much faster and to improve your effectiveness in implementing what you have learned. These resources are listed throughout the book as well as in Appendix A for easy reference. Of course, I would welcome the opportunity to work with you on implementing this system in your consulting firm. To reach me personally, please visit *MichaelMoshiri.com/work-with-michael*.

The Client Catalyst System is an efficient, predictable, and repeatable means for identifying highly qualified clients and connecting with them in a way that demonstrates your character, commitment, and competence. With a minimal investment of time, you can master this system, find high-quality prospective clients when you need them, and never chase clients again.

Wishing you the best of success.

Appendix A: Summary of Online Resources

This appendix provides a summary of the online resources, as well as products and services that can help you to execute and implement the strategies, ideas, and systems that you learn here in your consulting firm.

The relevant resources for each chapter of the book are listed below.

Chapter One

- NeverChaseClientsAgain.com/LeadGenEval: Download a complementary *Lead Generation Evaluation Worksheet* to evaluate the efficiency and effectiveness of your current lead generation techniques, and to focus your time and efforts on those techniques that provide you with the highest returns.

- NeverChaseClientsAgain.com/DISC: Obtain a special report to help you learn and apply the essential principles of the DISC Behavioral Styles method for identifying an individual's inherent communication, motivation, and learning preferences.
- NeverChaseClientsAgain.com/SoftSkills: Learn about the Seven Essential Soft Skills, evaluate your proficiency (or that of your consulting staff), and obtain additional resources and training programs related to these skills.
- NeverChaseClientsAgain.com/CoreTraining: Obtain proficiency evaluations and training resources related to the Three Core Qualifications of character, commitment, and competence that lead a prospective client to choose you and your firm over your competitors time and time again.

Chapter Three

- NeverChaseClientsAgain.com/BookBonuses: Gain access to additional resources such as checklists, templates, and worksheets to help you to save time and effort when implementing the Client Catalyst System.

Chapter Four

- NeverChaseClientsAgain.com/ClientQualChecklist: Download a complementary *Client Qualification Checklist* to save time when defining your PATRONS Criteria in Step 1 of the Client Catalyst System.
- NeverChaseClientsAgain.com/GoogleCheatSheet: Download a complementary *Google Search Cheat Sheet* and sample advanced "search strings" to use in your online search in Step 1 of the Client Catalyst System.

Chapter Five

- NeverChaseClientsAgain.com/IngressChecklist: Download a complementary *INGRESS Checklist* to save time when researching your potential pool of Catalysts among the Seven Sources of INGRESS.
- NeverChaseClientsAgain.com/DISC: Obtain a special report to help you learn and apply the essential principles of the DISC Behavioral Styles method for identifying your potential Catalyst's inherent communication, motivation, and learning preferences.

Chapter Six

- NeverChaseClientsAgain.com/FirstContact: Download a complimentary copy of the latest inventory of successful approaches, as well as sample e-mail messages that you can use to initiate contact with your chosen Catalyst in Step 3 of the Client Catalyst System.

Chapter Seven

- NeverChaseClientsAgain.com/CatalystMeeting: Download a complementary *Catalyst Meeting Checklist* to help you to successfully prepare for, orchestrate, and conduct your initial meeting with a potential Catalyst.
- NeverChaseClientsAgain.com/FirstContact: Download a complimentary copy of the latest inventory of successful approaches for initiating contact with your prospective clients in Step 4 of the Client Catalyst System.

Chapter Nine

- NeverChaseClientsAgain.com/Training: Access an online training course that can help you to avoid common mistakes and time-consuming trial and error in implementing the Client Catalyst System.
- NeverChaseClientsAgain.com/LeadersForum: Avoid the pain and frustration of learning through trial and error by joining a private community of firm leaders, seasoned consultants, and your peers who are interested in learning from each other as they build and grow their consulting firms.

Chapter Ten

- MichaelMoshiri.com/work-with-michael: Reach me personally to discuss working together on implementing the Client Catalyst System in your consulting firm.

Appendix B:
The Client Catalyst System Quick Reference

This appendix provides a summary of the steps that comprise the Client Catalyst System. For easy reference, the numbers associated with the steps listed below are identical to those used in the corresponding chapters in the book.

1. **Establish Criteria (Chapter Four)**
    - 1.1. Identify Your PATRONS
    - 1.2. Verify Your Criteria
        - 1.2.1. Search for Organizations
        - 1.2.2. Search for Professionals
    - 1.3. Commit to Your PATRONS
        - 1.3.1. Make a Public Commitment
2. **Evaluate Catalysts (Chapter Five)**

- 2.1. Search for Catalysts
  - 2.1.1. Begin with the Seven Sources of INGRESS
  - 2.1.2. Identify Potential Catalysts
- 2.2. Select the Most Qualified Catalysts
  - 2.2.1. Understand Catalyst Qualifications
  - 2.2.2. Evaluate Potential Catalysts

3. **Engage Catalysts (Chapter Six)**
   - 3.1. Facilitate Access to Your Catalysts
     - 3.1.1. Find a Contact Who Knows Your Catalyst
     - 3.1.2. Ask Your Contact for Advice
     - 3.1.3. Ask for Permission to Mention Names
   - 3.2. Develop an Offering of PURE Value
   - 3.3. Present Your Offering of PURE Value to Catalysts
   - 3.4. Verify Catalyst's Qualifications and Intent

4. **Elevate Yourself (Chapter Seven)**
   - 4.1. Identify Highly Qualified Clients
   - 4.2. Develop an Offering of PURE Value
     - 4.2.1. Think REMARKABLE
     - 4.2.2. Consult Your Catalyst
   - 4.3. Present Your Offering to Your Prospective Client
   - 4.4. Verify Client's Perception of Value

5. **Explore Opportunities (Chapter Eight)**
   - 5.1. Explore Opportunities to Serve Prospective Client
   - 5.2. Explore Opportunities to Connect with Others

Notes

Chapter Two

Wallace, Ed (2009). Business Relationships That Last: Five Steps to Transform Contacts into High Performing Relationships (Kindle Locations 689-690). Greenleaf Book Group LLC. Kindle Edition.

Chapter Seven

Maister, David (2008). Strategy And The Fat Smoker: Doing What's Obvious But Not Easy (p. 20). The Spangle Press.

Chapter Ten

Cialdini, Robert B. (1984). Influence: The Psychology of Persuasion (p. 13) HarperCollins Publishers Inc.

Index

A

Actions. *See* Offering
alliance, 103, 116
as an Offering, 116
Analog networking. *See* Networking
Associations. *See* Seven Sources of INGRESS
Authenticity. *See* Five Critical Character Traits
applicable to firms, 40
bravery and, 41
honesty with oneself and, 40

B

Beating the Competition. *See* Offering

C

Catalyst, 80, 84, 98, 117, 138
acting as door opener, 84
breadth and depth of network, 89
consulting on Offerings of PURE Value, 117
definition, 81

function in Seven Sources of INGRESS, 87
Gaining access to, 98
gathering information about, 99
importance of availability, 90
in-depth knowledge, 89
interim, 98, 99, 100, 101, 102, 130
maintaining relationship with, 138
personal interaction with, 93
pool of potential, 87
respected, 89
role in client community, 84
strength of relationships, 89
the most important qualification of, 92
well-connected, 89
why use one, 81
Catalyst Qualifications. *See* Seven Catalyst Qualifications
CLIENT. *See* Six Catalyst Advantages
Client Catalyst System, 18, 59, 60, 63, 66, 71, 72, 80, 82, 83, 84, 93, 98, 106, 110, 111, 113, 126, 127, 128, 129, 130, 137, 138, 139, 140, 144, 145, 148
Elevate Yourself, 62, 109
Engage Catalysts, 62, 97
Establish Criteria, 61, 65
Evaluate Catalysts, 61, 79
Explore Opportunities, 63, 125, 126
Commit, 126, 129
Engage, 126
Envision, 126, 128
Frame, 126, 128
Listen, 126, 127
offering professional services, 129
implementing as a team, 140
mistakes in implementing, 140
Step 1, 65
Step 2, 79
Step 3, 97
Step 4, 109
Step 5, 125
training course, 137
Clients
actively listening to, 127
challenging your fees, 37
chasing wrong clients, 28
demanding, 37

expectations
  setting and meeting, 42
Highly Qualified, 29
  criteria. *See* PATRONS Criteria
  identifying, 110
  defining, 66
holding back, 37
likability and choosing consultants, 47
management style, 69
micromanaging, 37
motivating to share issues, 127
needs, 69
  symptoms, 69
needs alignment, 30
refusing to give referrals, 37
what they look for, 31
why they choose you, 35
work ethics, 69
Consultative Skills. *See* Three Core Qualifications
consulting staff
behavior and client perception, 39
commitments to clients, 43
disconnect between firm leadership and, 74

Hard Skills, 50
high turnover rates in, 30
performance, 45
personal values, 43
Soft Skills, 52
Three Core Qualifications training, 54
training, 39, 53
credibility, 36, 39, 40, 41, 42, 45, 54, 60, 144, 145

D

Digital networking. *See* Networking

E

Elevate Yourself. *See* Client Catalyst System
Emotional Fulfillment. *See* Offering
Empathy. *See* Five Critical Character Traits
endorsement, 100, 106, 112, 122
Engage Catalysts. *See* Client Catalyst System
Enthusiasm. *See* Five Critical Character Traits
Establish Criteria. *See* Client Catalyst System

Evaluate Catalysts. *See* Client Catalyst System

Expansion Ideas. *See* Offering

Explore Opportunities. *See* Client Catalyst System

F

Five Critical Character Traits, 39

Authenticity, 39, 40
  demonstrating, 40
  questions to evaluate, 41

Empathy, 40, 43, 44, 91
  demonstrating, 43
  questions to evaluate, 44

Enthusiasm, 40, 45
  demonstrating, 45

Integrity, 39, 42
  demonstrating, 42
  questions to evaluate, 42
  the key to demonstrating, 42

Likability, 40, 46
  questions to evaluate, 47

Five Ps of Consulting, 52, 53

G

generating revenue
  focus on, 30
  gifts of knowledge, 103, 116

Groups and Associations. *See* Seven Sources of INGRESS

H

Hard Skills. *See* Three Core Qualifications

Highly Qualified. *See* Clients

I

influence, 44, 46, 83, 85, 89, 139, 145

Influence Centers. *See* Seven Sources of INGRESS

INGRESS. *See* Seven Sources of INGRESS

Integrity. *See* Five Critical Character Traits

interim Catalyst. *See* Catalyst

K

Knowledge
  as an Offering, 115

L

lead generation, 15, 18, 25, 27, 28, 143, 144
content marketing, 13, 15, 18, 27, 143
investing time in, 27
leveraging social media, 28
online, 28
social media, 13, 15, 18, 25, 26, 27, 28, 73, 75, 93, 143
techniques, 28
Leads. *See* Offering
Likability. *See* Five Critical Character Traits
LinkedIn, 26, 86, 93, 99

M

Major Interests. *See* Offering

N

Name Recognition. *See* Six Catalyst Advantages
Networking
Analog, 26
Digital, 25, 26
News and Information Sources. *See* Seven Sources of INGRESS

O

Offering
avoiding ineffective, 117
Catalyst feedback on, 118
definition, 101
examples, 101
perceived value of, 101
personal nature of, 101
REMARKABLE, 113, 114, 117
 Actions, 113, 115
 Alliances, 113, 116
 Beating the Competition, 114, 116
 Emotional Fulfillment, 113, 114
 Expansion Ideas, 114, 116
 Knowledge, 113, 115
 Leads, 114, 116
 Major Interests, 113, 115
 Relationships, 113, 114
 Revenue Ideas, 113, 115
Offering of PURE Value. *See* PURE Value

P

PATRONS Criteria, 66, 69, 70, 71, 72, 73, 74, 75, 110, 111, 145, 146
  Authority, 66, 67, 70, 73
    Decision Authority, 67
    Signing Authority, 67
  committing to, 73
  Needs, 66, 69
  Organization, 66, 68, 72
  Purchasing Power, 66, 67, 70, 72
  Roles and Responsibilities, 66, 68, 73
  Style, 66, 69
  Timing, 30, 66, 68, 70, 82, 84
  verifying, 71
Personal Intelligence, 83, 84, 89, 99, 100, 101, 102, 111, 113, 118, 119, 121, 144
Potential Catalysts. *See* Catalyst
professional relationships, 31, 32, 36, 144, 145
Soft Skills and, 51
PURE Value, 100, 103, 104, 105, 106, 107, 110, 111, 112, 113, 114, 117, 118, 119, 120, 126, 144, 145, 146
  consulting Catalysts about, 117
  definition, 101
  developing an Offering of, 100, 113
  examples, 102
  monetary value of, 103
  presenting to Catalysts, 104
    retaining control, 104
    three-step process, 104
  presenting to prospective clients, 118
    approaches to, 120
    persistence in, 121
    preparing for, 119
    retaining control, 119
    verifying client perception of value, 120

R

Referral and Networking Resources. *See* Seven Sources of INGRESS
referrals, 37, 74, 81, 82
  using incorrectly, 81
Relationships. *See* Offering

REMARKABLE. *See* Offering
Revenue Ideas. *See* Offering
RFP processes, 27

S

Service Providers. *See* Seven Sources of INGRESS
Seven Catalyst Qualifications, 88, 105, 107, 130
Available, 88, 90
Connected, 88, 89
Dependable, 88, 91
Inclined, 88, 90
Knowledgeable, 88
Relatable, 88, 91
Respected, 88, 89
the most important qualification of, 92
verifying, 105
Seven Essential Soft Skills training, 52
Seven Sources of INGRESS, 85, 86, 92
as knowledge hubs, 86
Events, Meetings and Conferences, 86
Groups and Associations, 85
identifying potential Catalysts and, 87
Influence Centers, 85
News and Information Sources, 85
Referral and Networking Resources, 85
Service Providers, 86
Social Networks and Forums, 86
Six Catalyst Advantages, 82, 89
Connections, 82
Evaluations, 82, 83
Intelligence, 82, 83
Levers, 82, 83
Name Recognition, 82, 84, 89
Timing, 82, 84
Social Networks and Forums. *See* Seven Sources of INGRESS
Soft Skills. *See* Three Core Qualifications

T

Three Core Qualifications, 21, 35, 36, 37, 38, 49, 54, 60, 62, 139, 140
Character, 36, 38, 139
associations between actions and, 39

Character Traits. *See* Five Critical Character Traits
Commitment, 47, 74
  demonstrating, 47
  selfish intent and, 47
Competence, 49
  Consultative Skills, 49, 52, 53
    questions to evaluate, 53
  Hard Skills, 49, 50, 51, 52
    client perception and, 50
    demonstrating, 50
    emphasis on, 51
  Soft Skills, 49, 51, 52, 53, 139
    building professional relationships and, 51

credibility and, 36
symptoms of failure to demonstrate, 37, 54
training, 54
training
  Client Catalyst System, 137
  Consultative Skills, 53
  Soft Skills, 52
  Three Core Qualifications, 54, 139
trust, 14, 36, 39, 40, 41, 45, 54, 60, 118, 144, 145

V

Value Levers, 111, 113, 118, 119, 121, 122, 144, *See* Six Catalyst Advantages
Value Questions, 48
  answering for existing clients, 49

About the Author

With over 20 years of experience in building and growing consulting practices and in leading client services at global firms such as Deloitte, EY, and PwC, Michael is widely considered an expert in business development and client relationship management in the consulting industry. Michael's clients have included some of the world's largest and most-recognized brands such as Pepsi, IBM, Wells Fargo, Visa, Nike, Microsoft, and Callaway Golf.

Michael is the International #1 Bestselling author of "Never Chase Clients Again," which provides consultants and consulting firm leaders with a proven system for finding, attracting, and winning highly qualified clients with minimal effort.

A dynamic speaker, Michael's presentations have helped myriad consultants and firm leaders around the world to build strong client relationships, increase their revenues, and build profitable consulting practices.

Michael has traveled to and empowered professionals to grow their consulting firms in 48 countries around the world, including England, Italy, France, Spain, Austria, Germany, Switzerland, Canada, Mexico, Colombia, South Africa, Australia, Dubai, Iran, India, China, Philippines, and Japan.

Michael lives with his family in Phoenix, Arizona. He is an avid reader, a passionate rugby fan, and an aspiring marksman. For more information about Michael, visit MichaelMoshiri.com.

CPSIA information can be obtained at www.ICGtesting.com
Printed in the USA
LVOW07*1309171115

462969LV00003B/6/P